MW00415205

A I   H A R M O N Y

Blending Human Expertise and AI

for Business Success

Brad Flaugher

PIERUCCI
PUBLISHING

Copyright © Brad Flaugher, 2023
AI Harmony
Blending Human Expertise and AI for Business Success By Brad Flaugher

Published by Pierucci Publishing, P.O. Box 2074, Carbondale, Colorado 81623, USA
www.pieruccipublishing.com

Cover design by Angela Altamirano and Brad Flaugher
Edited by Russell Womack

Hardcover ISBN: 978-1-956257-82-3
eBook ISBN: 978-1-956257-81-6

Library of Congress Control Number: 2023909932

All rights reserved. Except as permitted under U.S. Copyright Act of 1976, no part of this publication may be reproduced, distributed or transmitted in any form or by any means, or stored in a database or retrieval system without the prior written permission of the copyright owner. The scanning, uploading and distribution of this book via the Internet or via any other means without the permission of the author is illegal and punishable by law. Thank you for purchasing only authorized electronic editions, and for withdrawing your consent or approval for electronic piracy of copyrightable materials. Your support of the author's rights, as well as your own integrity is appreciated.

Pierucci Publishing books may be purchased in bulk at special discounts for sales promotion, corporate gifts, fund-raising, or educational purposes. Special editions can be created to specifications. For details, contact the Special Sales Department, Pierucci Publishing, PO Box 2074, Carbondale, CO 81623 or Support@PierucciPublishing.com or toll-free telephone at 1-855-720-1111.

*To the visionary mentors who unraveled
the enigma of mathematical chaos,
kindling the flames of lucidity
in the realms of modeling and AI.*

FOREWORD

Brad Flaugher's book *AI Harmony: Blending Human Expertise And AI For Business Success* has a clear goal. The author wants people to be convinced that the new Artificial Intelligence (AI) will be an indispensable tool for the remaining part of the 21st century.

AI Harmony has two parts. The first four chapters review the transition from classical AI (often called Good Old-Fashioned Artificial Intelligence - GOFAI) to the deep learning models without going into historical and technical details. The second part briefly specifies the scope and limits of two dozen exciting applications, many of which are in the author's close interest.

AI is the study of how to make computers do things at which people are initially better. AI is now a buzzword, and everybody is interested in how large, creative AI models will transform our lives and labor markets. As we know, there is nothing new under the Sun. Alan Turing, in a celebrated 1950 paper (Computing Machinery and Intelligence) described what is now called "The Turing Test". The Turing Test is a challenge to determine if a computer can demonstrate human-like intelligence by having a conversation with a person that's so convincing, the person can't tell they're talking to a machine. Turing predicted that in about fifty years, "an average interrogator will not have more than a 70 percent chance of making the right identification after five minutes of questioning." (Turing 1997, 29-32).

Formal AI started with the Dartmouth Conference in 1956. As the organizers claimed,

We propose that a 2 month, 10 man study of artificial intelligence be carried out during the summer of 1956 at Dartmouth College in Hanover, New Hampshire. The study is to proceed on the basis of the conjecture that every aspect of learning or any other feature of intelligence can in principle be so precisely described that a machine can be made to simulate it?[1]

Alan Newell and Herbert Simon, two of the most important pioneers of (GOF) AI and cognitive science, predicted in 1957, "Within ten years a computer will be the world's chess champion unless the rules bar it from competition." Their theory was based on the assumption that "A physical symbol system has the necessary and sufficient means of general intelligent action."[2]

Initially, AI used purely symbolic methods. Knowledge about the external world and problems are represented by logic and rules. Famously, Logic Theorist was a computer program written in 1956 by Newell, Simon, and Cliff Shaw. The program performed automated reasoning and has been labeled as "the first artificial intelligence program". The initial successes increased expectations and promises, which proved unrealistic, and funding dried, and the first AI Winter arrived. About a decade later the rise of expert systems implied a second boom.

The origin of the sub-symbolic approach goes back to McCulloch and Pitts, whose model in 1943 wanted to capture the logical structure of the nervous systems. The MCP model (i) introduced a formalism whose refinement and generalization led to the notion of finite automata (an essential concept in computability theory); (ii) is a technique that inspired the idea of logic design of computers; (iii) used first computational algorithms to examine the brain-mind problem, and (iv) offered the first modern computational theory of brain and mind.

---

1   http://jmc.stanford.edu/articles/dartmouth/dartmouth.pdf
2   Handbook of Research on Emerging Rule-Based Languages and Technologies: Open Solutions and Approaches." 2009, page 32

A new era started with the construction of Learning Machines. The Perceptron (around 1960) is a mathematical construction of an adaptive neural network able to learn and classify inputs. Rosenblatt defined it by adding to the MCP rule a learning rule to modify synaptic weights. Minsky and Papert proved in 1969 that a single-layer Perceptron could not solve the "exclusive OR" problem, since Perceptrons were assumed to be able to classify only linearly separable patterns. The implication of the critique was the severe restriction on funding neural network research. However, the analysis is not valid for multilayer neural networks. After introducing a new learning algorithm called backpropagation, the field of artificial neural networks became very popular. As it happens with fashions, there were ups and downs. Deep learning algorithms have become very useful in the last ten years. The adjective deep refers to the number of layers the data transforms into.

The considerable achievement of large language models has concurrently raised significant concerns regarding the potential for AI to learn and perform undesirable actions. As the author of this Foreword, my capabilities do not extend to prophesy; hence, I can only offer insights on anticipated developments and what may likely be absent.

I found very stimulating the second part of the book, which contain the brief specification of about two dozen case studies. The two most important classes of case studies are the Classifiers and the Predictors. Prediction is the output of an algorithm trained on a historical dataset and specifically applied to new data to forecasting the likelihood of a particular outcome. Classifiers are machine learning algorithms that automatically orders or categorizes data into one or more of a set of classes.

Examples for Classifiers on the book are:
Lithium Mining Site Classifier
Large NYSE Stock Order Classifier
Handwriting Classifier
Autism Classifier
The Online Ad Server Classifier
Fake News Classifier

Hate Speech Classifier
Smartwatch Danger Classifier
A number of applications of Predictors:
Models used in finance to predict the likelihood of a company's shares being purchased through a tender offer.
Horse Racing Prediction
Simple Credit Score (a type of machine learning model that's designed to predict an individual's creditworthiness)
Social Credit Score (a type of machine learning model that's designed to predict an individual's trustworthiness based on their social behavior and online activities)
The Artificial General Intelligence (AGI) Chatbot: type of machine learning model that's designed to simulate human-like conversation with users.

Self-driving cars and autonomous weapons are analyzed in separate chapters. The role of statistical models are emphasized in the future of transportation. The potential of artificial intelligence in the realm of warfare leads very far. Control theory should have a critical role in the development and application of autonomous weaponry.

The model descriptions are very useful. The Reader will learn how the training data were obtained, what are the limits and risks, how expensive its recreation might be, etc. Brad Flaugher convinces us that there is no medicine against progress. Deep learning, even if it not a silver bullet, will help us to integrate artificial and human intelligence.

Péter Érdi
Henry Luce Professor of Complex Systems Studies
Kalamazoo College,
Kalamazoo, MI
May 2023

ACKNOWLEDGEMENTS

I would like to express my deepest gratitude to Angela Altamirano for creating the wonderful cover art. Special thanks to Stephanie Pierucci and Russell Womack for their tireless efforts in publishing, and to Dan Bernard and Michael Townsend for their invaluable support with the audiobook.

My sincere appreciation goes to my early supporters: William Dickson, Daniel Hoevel, Patrick Maloney, Jerrod Howlett, and Jeff Zinser. A special thank you to Louis Cid and the Harvard Club of New York for providing me with an early forum. I am also grateful to the Data Meetup Philadelphia and Joe Eubel for their encouragement. Dr. Elisa Esposito deserves a heartfelt thank you for her constant support.

I would like to express my profound gratitude to Dr. Péter Érdi for taking me under his wing many years ago. I am also especially indebted to the following educators: Ron Conwell, Tim Leunig, Alyce Brady, Pam Cutter, and Cade Massey.

I would like to acknowledge my bootcamp students, your effort is inspiring and you all are certainly in the right field at the right time. Also my current and former colleagues: Liubomyr Pohreliuk, Davide Anastasia, Matthew Griffiths, Jonathan Bloch, and Anthony Lauzon for their invaluable insights and contributions.

Lastly, I would like to extend my gratitude to the open source software community and the Free Software Foundation. This book uses the kaobook LaTeX project and many Free and Open Source AI models for text and image generation like Stable Diffusion and Mann-E. Special thanks to the Linux Foundation, PyTorch Foundation, Google for Tensorflow, Meta and Yann Lecun for LLaMA, and OpenAI.

PREFACE

Welcome to *AI Harmony: Blending Human Expertise and AI for Business Success*. This book is a comprehensive guide that will help you understand how Artificial Intelligence (AI) works and how you can use it to your advantage. My goal is to provide you with a clear and unbiased understanding of AI, without the need for a technical background.

As you read through the chapters, you'll learn about how AI models are trained, with in-depth analysis of every common use case I believe is important. In chapter five, we'll delve into the specifics of AI training and explore how it can be used for business success. I've also dedicated entire chapters to the topics of autonomous weapons and self-driving cars, which I believe are important areas to consider when thinking about AI.

My hope is that this book will be useful to all readers, regardless of their role in the world of AI. Whether you're a user, developer, or investor in AI, there's something in here for you. Feel free to skip around and read the stories that interest you most – although I highly recommend the first four chapters as a must-read for everyone.

I've enjoyed writing this book, and I hope you'll enjoy reading it. And if you have any notes or feedback, please don't hesitate to reach out to me at brad@bradflaugher.com.

Remember, the goal of this book is not to be read from cover to cover, but to be used as a reference and guide for understanding AI. So take your time, read what interests you, and feel free to come back to other sections later.

Thank you for embarking on this journey with me. I hope you find this book informative, useful, and enjoyable.

Philadelphia, PA
Brad Flaugher
March 2023

TABLE OF CONTENTS

CHAPTER SUMMARIES

1
AI-enabled Mass Destruction

AI has the power to disrupt various aspects of our lives, and the democratization of AI is reducing the need for human labor, driving down the cost of creation. The adoption of AI is a gradual process that may take time to fully permeate our society, but its widespread adoption is probably unstoppable. To ensure that AI serves as a catalyst for progress, we should embrace it, create an "AI-positive" culture, and rewrite our work assignments accordingly.

2
The End of Good Old-Fashioned Artificial Intelligence

Avoid the term "AI" and instead differentiate between rules-based programming and deep learning to prevent confusion. Good Old-Fashioned AI (rules-based AI) is challenging to create and maintain, while modern deep learning techniques use data to train models and can be as good as the data they are trained with. Good Old-Fashioned AI is not well-suited for many complex tasks, like translation and object detection.

3
The Regression Theory of Everything

Deep learning models are large unscientific regression systems that map input data to output data. They are complex, deterministic, and exhibit chaotic behavior, making their inner workings functionally unknowable and difficult to test. Multicollinearity and feature importance can only be understood with a high level of statistical error. Getting good data to train with is crucial for machine learning engineers to train good models. While deep learning models can have impressive and useful outputs, it's important to acknowledge their failures and limitations, which can be encouraged by users, managers and investors.

4
Creativity and Decision Making with Deep Learning Models

Users should consider the quality and appropriateness of the data the model is trained on and ask questions about how and when the data was collected and cleaned up. Deep learning models are not sentient creative creatures and are deterministic systems that can only generate outputs based on their training data. Users should also avoid allowing models to do everything and manage the models cautiously and carefully.

5
Case Studies

A deep analysis of many popular machine learning models, from online dating, stock trading, threat detection, and more. To ensure transparency and accountability of AI models, it is important to create and use model cards that provide information on their capabilities and limitations. Avoid "sucker traps" like biased training sets, decision-making ability, and concept drift when analyzing models. Understanding the training data and allowing the model to give low-stakes advice can also be helpful. It's crucial to manage the model's performance and not give decision-making ability to all models.

6
Self-Driving with Statistics

The use of deep learning models in self-driving cars has limitations that require control and regulation. Future developments in infrastructure and control systems may support fully autonomous vehicles. Statistical models play a crucial role in the future of transportation and must be thoroughly understood to ensure safe and effective self-driving cars.

7
Unplugging Skynet

As we approach the artificial intelligence revolution, people's fears of machines taking over the world are largely unfounded, and the more immediate risks of economic disruption should be focused on. Intelligence does not generate a drive for domination, and survival instinct is not hardwired into AI. The real risk is AI leading to further increases in wealth and income inequalities unless new policies are implemented.

8
Revolutionary for Whom?

This chapter explores the various facets of AI and its role in the modern world. We discuss how AI assistants differ from traditional butlers and virtual assistants, and the limitations of AI-generated content. Emphasizing the importance of embracing AI in the workplace, we examine the rise of "organic content" and propose a framework for navigating AI's impact on careers. Addressing concerns about AI's "dead inside" nature, we stress the need to let AI excel at its tasks while humans focus on their unique strengths. Finally, we debunk common misconceptions surrounding AI's potential to replace humans and seize control of our civilization, advocating for the integration of AI as a powerful, complementary tool in our society.

1

AI-ENABLED MASS DESTRUCTION

There is little doubt that AI will contribute to profound transformations over the next decades. At its best, the technology has the potential to release us from mundane work and create a utopia in which all time is leisure time. At its worst, World War III might be fought by armies of superintelligent robots. But they won't be led by HAL, Skynet or their newer AI relatives. Even in the worst case, the robots will remain under our command, and we will have only ourselves to blame.
Yann LeCun & Anthony Zador 2019 [1]

1.1 The AI Renaissance

Technology often finds its first adopters among those who can afford it and foresee its potential. Artificial Intelligence (AI) is no exception with its early applications dating back several decades, notably in the financial industry. Hedge funds and investment banks identified the value of AI and started using it for trading and portfolio management.

Renaissance Technologies, a hedge fund founded by mathematician James Simons, exemplifies the early adoption of AI. Since 1978, the company has used AI to predict market movements and optimize trading strategies. By employing highly skilled PhDs known as "quants" to develop algorithms and AI models, Renaissance Technologies has become one of the most successful hedge funds in history.

As AI gained traction, tech giants like Google and Microsoft began investing in their own quants. These experts were tasked with using AI to address a wide range of challenges, from refining search algorithms to enhancing language processing capabilities. Much of this research was made public, allowing the broader community to benefit from these advancements. AI-enabled products became more visible to consumers, and AI tooling became very accessible to developers. Online advertising became a highly visible industry where AI is able to analyze user behavior and target ads with remarkable precision.

The accessibility of AI technology has increased thanks in part to open-source projects that enable individuals and smaller organizations to tap into its power. This democratization of AI has ignited a wave of innovation, with developers worldwide contributing to the AI renaissance. Developments in AI have turned a corner; large open-source datasets coupled with cheap computing power and powerful open-source development tools have taken AI out of the realm of expensive private enterprise into a new era where companies give away large and valuable models under strong public licenses (like Stable Diffusion from StabilityAI, LLaMA from Facebook) and the most innovative companies operate as large non-profit or limited-profit entities (like OpenAI, the creators of ChatGPT).

The world of open AI acknowledges that training data is valuable, but realizes that especially on the internet, information wants to be free. The risks of data theft and unauthorized use have been escalating, and the industry is simultaneously having its "iPhone moment" with the advent of ChatGPT and its "Napster Moment" with the public release of large generative models trained on copyrighted content[2]. Companies and individuals are striving to protect their intellectual property while others look for ways to exploit it; but if the past is a guide, copyright holders are likely to lose out as the ability to capture income from copyrighted content moves from content creators and to content distributors, namely large cloud computing companies that run AI models at scale.

This situation sets the stage for an AI copyright battle looming on the horizon. As the distinction between proprietary and open-source information blurs, the question of who owns AI-generated content becomes increasingly important. Governments, corporations, and individuals are all grappling with the legal and ethical implications of AI and its widespread adoption. When one considers that AI models themselves are content that can be modeled and stolen, one can get a glimpse of the full destructive and transformative power of AI. AI doesn't just allow you to benefit from copy written text and images and create your own that you can distribute. AI also allows you to copy the multibillion dollar models that researchers at Google, Microsoft, and Facebook have made, and modify and distribute them as long as you have the technical know-how and a big enough computer to run the models. The AI renaissance is breaking traditional business models and is also breaking the business models of its creators almost as soon as it is released. Like many transformative technologies, AI is shrinking the market, making things cheap for everyone, and capturing market share.

1.2   AI Shrinks the Market and Takes Market Share

The "Software Paradox" posits that as software becomes more open, it tends to shrink markets while capturing most of the market share. This phenomenon can be observed in the current state of AI, particularly with the advent of open-source AI. As AI technologies become more sophisticated and widespread, they are reducing the need for human labor in many markets, and bring the cost of creation down significantly across industries[3].

One key aspect of AI's impact on the market is its ability to automate repetitive and mundane tasks, thereby allowing humans to focus on more complex and creative aspects of their work. This not only streamlines processes, but also has the potential to improve the overall quality of work. With AI handling the less desirable tasks, human workers can concentrate on utilizing their unique skills and expertise, resulting in better outcomes and higher value-added work.

The rise of open-source AI further accelerates this trend, making advanced AI tools and algorithms accessible to a broader range of individuals and organizations. As these powerful tools become more widely available, businesses across various industries will find it increasingly difficult to justify the cost of employing human workers for tasks that can be more efficiently completed by AI. This shift will result in a smaller job market for those specific tasks, with AI taking the majority of the market share.

However, the shrinking of specific labor markets does not necessarily mean the eradication of all human work. Instead, it presents an opportunity for the workforce to adapt and focus on roles that are complementary to AI systems.

1.3   The Other Economy, the One Without AI

As AI revolutionizes various sectors of the economy, there's another economy that remains untouched by AI's transformative effects. This other economy is characterized by heavily regulated industries that often resist technological innovation, resulting in stagnating growth and rising costs for consumers[4].

In many places, AI is practically illegal. This is partly due to consumers, professional organizations, and governments struggling to keep up with the rapid pace of technological advancements, thereby leading to a lack of understanding and appropriate regulations[5]. Additionally, public opinion remains skeptical about the widespread adoption of AI, as evidenced by polls[6] [7]. This skepticism is not helped by stories of software developers becoming emotionally attached to AI chatbots[8].

The contrast between sectors that embrace AI and those that resist it highlights a growing divide in the economy. In industries where AI is allowed to flourish, technological innovation drives down prices and increases product quality, leading to a more efficient market. However, heavily regulated sectors that resist AI adoption experience rising costs and stagnating growth, ultimately consuming a larger share of the economy.

This phenomenon is exacerbated by the emotional interplay between production and consumption. As consumers, we tend to become frustrated with price increases in the heavily regulated sectors. On the other hand, as producers, we may feel threatened by technological disruption in industries that embrace AI. This dichotomy demonstrates the inherent conflict between the desire for stability in the economy and the need for innovation and progress.

As the regulated, non-technological sectors continue to grow as a percentage of GDP, the economy may ultimately become dominated by these stagnating industries. In such a scenario, the full potential of AI and other advanced technologies may never be realized. This highlights the importance of addressing regulatory barriers, fostering public understanding, and promoting AI adoption in industries that have yet to embrace its potential.

Undoubtedly, individuals seeking to leverage AI for their professional tasks will do so, and it is crucial to establish appropriate controls and governance in anticipation of this shift. As high school assignments across the nation undergo transformation, so too will the nature of our work. Fortunately for humankind, many of these assignments that are being restructured were inherently flawed to begin with. In the era of virtual communication, we identified gatherings that could have been condensed into emails. Now, we are poised to uncover occupations that could have been efficiently managed through simple prompts given to an AI.

By fostering an "AI-positive" culture of collaboration and transparency, we can ensure that AI serves as a catalyst for progress rather than a hindrance. Ultimately, the key to unlocking AI's full potential lies in our ability to navigate the delicate balance between innovation and regulation, embracing the opportunities for growth while addressing the inherent risks and concerns that come with this new era of technological advancement.

1.4   (Human and AI) Workers of The World, Unite!

AI's adoption can be seen as an extension of the outsourcing trend that has been prevalent for decades. The principle "if you can't beat them, join them" seems more relevant than ever as people increasingly integrate AI into their work and lives.

Even in places where AI is technically illegal or frowned upon, individuals find creative ways to leverage AI to make their lives easier. Students may use AI to help write essays, office workers may employ Optical Character Recognition (OCR) to avoid tedious data entry tasks, and programmers might utilize GitHub Copilot regardless of whether their employers approve. These examples demonstrate that as AI tools become more accessible and affordable, they will infiltrate various industries.

Instead of resisting this trend, we should work with it and guide its development. Embracing AI and integrating it into our work processes can lead to increased productivity, innovation, and overall improvement in our quality of life [9]. The situation with AI usage is reminiscent of self-driving cars and semi-autonomous driving modes. Despite manufacturers' intentions and guidelines, these features are often treated as fully autonomous by users, reflecting the human tendency to push boundaries and adapt technology to suit their needs.

As AI becomes more ingrained in our daily lives, it's essential to recognize the inevitability of its adoption and focus on guiding its development in a way that maximizes its benefits and minimizes potential risks. By uniting human and AI workers, we can foster a collaborative environment that leverages the strengths of both entities and paves the way for a more efficient, innovative, and prosperous future [10].

If we learn any lessons from early adopters of AI in finance, we'll learn that humans role has changed, but not disappeared. *"There was a time when everyone thought the quants had figured it out. That is not the perception today. When it comes to the stockmarket, at least, automation has not been the winner-takes-all event that many fear elsewhere. It is more like a tug-of-war between humans and machines. And though the machines are winning, humans have not let go just yet."* [11]

1.5   An AI Sherlock Holmes?

In an intimate conversation around the proverbial fireplace in 2023, NVIDIA's CEO, Jensen Huang, engaged in a spirited dialogue with Ilya Sutskever, a luminary in the realm of artificial intelligence and co-creator of ChatGPT. Sutskever likened the advancements in generative AI to handing the machine an enigmatic mystery tale, challenging it to decipher the climactic revelation: "the killer is... [blank]." He postulated that an AI adept at unearthing the final word of the whodunit may possess some semblance of comprehension and reasoning, effectively "compressing" its understanding of the world.

In this literary endeavor, we shall embark on an in-depth journey to discern the extent of AI's capacity for reasoning, the limits of its abilities, the intricacies of its creation, and the judicious application of its power. Grasping the answers to these pivotal inquiries is paramount to appreciating the role AI ought to play in our existence. Should we perceive AI as merely a "blurry JPEG of the Web," [12] and if ChatGPT is doing any compression of its knowledge what is lost? And what should humans add back before making decisions? Should we worry? Or should we envision AI as a digital Sherlock Holmes, wielding the formidable power of boundless deduction?

1.6   Is it The Future Yet?

Artificial intelligence (AI), as a general-purpose technology, has the potential to transform various aspects of our lives. However, its widespread adoption and impact on Total Factor Productivity (TFP) might not happen overnight. History has shown that even groundbreaking general-purpose technologies can take time to reach their full potential.

Take electricity, for example. Although Thomas Edison invented the light bulb in 1879, it took several decades for electricity to become the primary power source in industries and households. The infrastructure required to generate and distribute electricity on a large scale was built gradually, and businesses needed time to adapt their processes and machinery to leverage this new energy source. It wasn't until the early 20th century that the true impact of electricity on productivity and economic growth was realized.

Another example is the steam engine, invented by James Watt in 1775, which marked the beginning of the Industrial Revolution. The technology's full potential was not realized until several decades later. The adoption of steam-powered machinery required significant investments in infrastructure and the reorganization of production processes. Additionally, the development of railway networks and steamships expanded the reach of this technology, leading to a profound impact on productivity and global trade.

The internet also followed a similar pattern. While the internet was conceived in the late 1960s, it wasn't until the 1990s that its commercial potential began to be explored. The widespread adoption of the internet required the development of user-friendly web browsers, the expansion of telecommunications infrastructure, and the emergence of e-commerce platforms. It took several years for the internet to become an integral part of our daily lives and contribute to increased productivity across various industries.

So, while AI has the potential to revolutionize numerous aspects of our lives, it may take time for this technology to fully permeate our society and yield its maximum benefits. Patience and continuous innovation will be essential in realizing the transformative potential of AI. By learning from the history of general-purpose technologies, we can better understand the trajectory AI might follow and work toward a future where it significantly impacts productivity and our everyday lives.

1.7   Key Takeaways

▶ **AI is a general-purpose technology that possesses the potential to disrupt various aspects of our lives, including the job market and the economy.** This power to creatively destroy should not be underestimated as it can bring about significant transformations.

▶ **The democratization of AI has effectively reduced the cost of creation to close to zero.** Open-source developers worldwide are contributing to the AI revolution. The rise of open-source AI is gradually reducing the need for human labor in many markets, thereby significantly driving down the cost of creation across various industries.

▶ **The adoption of AI is not a new phenomenon; it is merely an extension of the outsourcing trend that has been prevalent for decades.** The shift toward automation has been a gradual process and is unlikely to happen overnight.

▶ **The pace of technological change is often slower than what the news may suggest.** While AI has the potential to revolutionize numerous aspects of our lives, it may take time for this technology to fully permeate our society and yield its maximum benefits.

▶ **AI's widespread adoption is probably unstoppable, given its affordability and its ability to operate stealthily.** Rather than resisting this shift, we must embrace it and work to determine how humans can best fit into this new era. By creating an "AI-positive" culture of collaboration and transparency, we can ensure that AI serves as a catalyst for progress. Just like in finance where machines have "taken over," there is still room for human traders, risk managers, etc. In the same way, we should now assume that every worker and student will use AI going forward and rewrite our assignments accordingly.

THE END OF GOOD OLD-FASHIONED ARTIFICIAL INTELLIGENCE

"Programming will be obsolete. I believe the conventional idea of "writing a program" is headed for extinction, and indeed, for all but very specialized applications, most software, as we know it, will be replaced by AI systems that are trained rather than programmed. In situations where one needs a "simple" program (after all, not everything should require a model of hundreds of billions of parameters running on a cluster of GPUs), those programs will, themselves, be generated by an AI rather than coded by hand."
Matt Welsh, 2023[13]

2.1 The AI Textbook of Yore

The widely used AI textbook, Artificial Intelligence, published in 1983 was a groundbreaking work that played a pivotal role in establishing numerous core concepts and techniques in the field of artificial intelligence (AI). However, the rapid advancements in AI over the past few decades have rendered many chapters in this renowned textbook outdated..

One of the main reasons for this is the prevalence of deep learning, big data, and large-scale statistical models in modern AI. These techniques have largely replaced the symbolic, rule-based approach to AI that was emphasized in the textbook, making many of the chapters on knowledge representation and expert systems less relevant.

Additionally, the explosion of data and the availability of powerful computing resources have made it possible to apply machine learning techniques at a scale that was previously unimaginable. This has led to the development of highly effective machine learning models that can handle complex tasks such as image and speech recognition with a high degree of accuracy, making many of the chapters on simpler machine learning techniques such as decision trees and linear regression less relevant [14].

We'll discuss this history and a few examples from the "early days" of AI to help us understand where we are headed. We'll start with machine translation, and then discuss chess and finally neural networks, which will be the focus of the rest of this book.

2.2 Explicit Rules and Codified Human Knowledge

When we "teach" a computer to perform a task by explicitly writing down all of the rules of that task, we are really codifying human understanding. When we codify human understanding, we write down every rule that we know explicitly. For small tasks, we can do this with 100 percent accuracy, and only minor headaches on the part of the software developer.

For example, let's write a boring function to tell you the number of days for a given month.

```python
def days_in_month(year,month):
    if month in [1, 3, 5, 7, 8, 10, 12]:
        return 31
    elif month in [4, 6, 9, 11]:
        return 30
    elif month== 2:
        if (year% 4 == 0 and year% 100 != 0) or year% 400 == 0:
            return 29
```

```
else:
    return 28
else:
    return "Invalidmonth"
```

Writing code can be a tedious and repetitive task, especially when it comes to debugging and testing. It can be especially frustrating when you're working on a large project and you're trying to track down a specific bug that's causing the program to crash. Testing code can also be boring as it often involves running the same tests over and over again to ensure that the code is working correctly.

Additionally, writing code can be boring because it requires a lot of concentration and focus. It can be easy to get lost in the details and lose track of time, especially if you're working on a complex problem. It can also be challenging to come up with creative solutions to problems, and it can be frustrating when your code doesn't work as expected.

While writing and testing code can be rewarding and fulfilling, it can also be a tedious and boring process. It requires a lot of patience, persistence, and attention to detail, and it can be easy to get frustrated and lose motivation. However, with practice and perseverance, it is possible to overcome these challenges and find enjoyment in the process of writing and testing code.

AI has traditionally operated by explicitly codifying human knowledge into machine-readable formats by doing the boring job of coding. This approach, which I'm calling "codified human knowledge" relies on humans to carefully structure and organize information in a way that can be understood by the AI system. The AI system then uses this structured knowledge to make decisions and perform tasks.

However, recent advances in AI have largely ignored the knowledge representation problem and instead have focused on using statistical techniques and neural networks to automatically learn patterns and relationships in data. This approach, known as "deep learning," involves training large neural networks on vast amounts of data, allowing the AI system to make educated classifications and transformations of data without explicit human guidance.

Deep learning has proven to be highly effective in a variety of applications, such as image and speech recognition, and has contributed to the rapid progress we have seen in AI in recent years. However, the reliance on large amounts of data and the lack of transparency in these models can make it difficult to understand how they are making decisions, which can be a concern in certain applications (especially Self-Driving and National Defense, see chapters 6 and 7).

2.3 IBM Tries Every Possible Chess Move

Deep Blue was a revolutionary computer developed by IBM that was specifically designed to play chess at the highest level. It was programmed with a vast database of chess knowledge and was able to analyze millions of positions per second.

Garry Kasparov was the reigning world chess champion at the time, and he was considered to be one of the greatest players in history. He was beaten by Deep Blue, which used rules-based GOFAI (Good Old Fashioned AI) to essentially calculate every possible move and project that move to the end of the game, then choose the best position by brute force. Despite Kasparov's best efforts, he was no match for Deep Blue's computational power. In the end, Deep Blue emerged victorious, defeating Kasparov in a historic match that changed the world of chess forever.

Deep Blue was a turning point in the development of AI, but Deep Blue's methods (namely calculating every possible outcome of a chess game to determine the best move) was not suitable for many of the world's problems. It turns out that chess is fun, but the world is not like chess. The "real" future of AI was being developed elsewhere, using statistics and a toy model of the brain to solve a very practical problem for banks.

2.4   Statistical Analysis of Handwriting is the Way of the Future

In the early 1990s, Yann LeCun was a researcher at Bell Labs in New Jersey. At the time, the process of reading and processing checks was a tedious and time-consuming task that was done manually by bank employees. LeCun saw the potential for using artificial intelligence to automate this process, and he began experimenting with using convolutional neural networks (CNNs) to recognize patterns in images of checks.

At the time, CNNs were a relatively new type of neural network that had been developed in the 1980s for image recognition tasks. They were inspired by the structure of the human visual system, and were able to process images in a way that was similar to how the human brain does.

LeCun's work was groundbreaking, and he was able to achieve impressive results using CNNs to process checks. By 1993, he had developed a system that was able to read and process checks with a high degree of accuracy, significantly reducing the amount of time and effort that was required to process checks manually.

LeCun's work on using CNNs for check processing was a major milestone in the field of artificial intelligence, and it laid the foundation for the development of many other applications of CNNs in the years that followed. Today, CNNs are widely used in a variety of applications, including facial recognition, image classification, and natural language processing.

2.5   Less Programmer Intelligence and More Data Intelligence

I think it's useful to separate the knowledge in the AI problem-space into two groups. The data and the programmer together make the programs that we use every day, and for the rest of this book I'll try and separate the discussion of the smarts of each to help us better understand the world.

Early AI relied heavily on a human programmer to design, write, and debug computer programs. Good programmers needed domain expertise, problem-solving skills, logical thinking, and the ability to learn and adapt to new programming languages and technologies.

We are now in the age of big data, and everyone knows that "data is gold". Statistical AI methods that are now most prevalent rely on extracting meaningful insights and knowledge from large datasets. This involves using statistical and analytical methods to discover patterns and trends in data, and using this information to inform business decisions or solve problems.

Throughout this book, I'll discuss the interaction between programmers and data, and what can go wrong. Working with big data and statistics at a large scale has given AI tremendous ability, but has made understanding and testing models infinitely more difficult. It is your author's belief that understanding the nuance of this interaction between programmer and data is essential to understanding modern AI.

2.6   From Explicit Rules to a Black Box, and Beyond

Artificial intelligence (AI) has come a long way since its inception, and the way that it makes decisions has changed significantly over time. In the early days of AI, explicit rules were used to tell the AI system what to do in certain situations. These rules were often written by humans and encoded into the system, and the AI would follow them to make decisions.

However, with the advent of deep learning, we have started to rely on a statistical understanding of the truth for AI to make decisions. Deep learning is a type of machine learning that involves training artificial neural networks on large datasets. These neural networks are able to learn patterns and relationships in the data, and can use this knowledge to make decisions.

The use of deep learning has led to the development of powerful AI that is able to perform tasks that were previously thought to be impossible for a machine to handle. For example, deep learning has led to the development of AI systems that are able to recognize faces, translate languages, and even beat humans at complex games like chess and Go.

While deep learning has led to significant advances in AI, it has also made it harder to debug and understand how the AI system is making its decisions. With explicit rules, it was relatively easy to understand why the AI made a particular decision. However, with deep learning, it is often difficult to understand exactly how the AI arrived at its decision. This can make it challenging to troubleshoot problems with the AI system and to ensure that it is making decisions that are fair and unbiased.

AI has come a long way since its early days, and the way that it makes decisions has changed significantly over time. While explicit rules were once used to tell the AI what to do, we now rely on a statistical understanding of the truth for AI to make decisions. This has led to the development of powerful AI that is able to perform a wide range of tasks, but it has also made it harder to debug and understand how the AI is making its decisions.

2.7 Key Takeaways

- **AI is a misleading term,** we should instead talk about rules-based programming (GOFAI) and deep learning so we don't confuse ourselves, our partners and our users.

- Good Old-Fashioned AI **(rules-based AI) is hard to create and maintain**. We used to use it for chess engines (like Deep Blue) and translation, but now programmers favor using statistical machine learning techniques.

- Good Old-Fashioned AI is not well suited to many problems, like machine translation and handwriting detection.

- Modern Deep Learning techniques use data to train models instead of humans explicitly writing rules, and the **deep learning models are often as good as the data they are trained with.**

3

THE REGRESSION THEORY

OF EVERYTHING

"AI Scientists disagree as to whether these language networks possess
true knowledge or are just mimicking humans by remembering
the statistics of millions of words. I don't believe any kind of deep
learning network will achieve the goal of AGI [Artificial General
Intelligence] if the network doesn't model the world the way the brain
does. Deep learning networks work well, but not because they solved
the knowledge representation problem. They work well because they
avoided it completely, relying on statistics and lots of data instead. How
deep learning networks work is clever, their performance impressive,
and they are commercially valuable. I am only pointing out that they
don't possess knowledge and, therefore, are not on the path to having
the ability of a five-year-old child."
Jeff Hawkins, 2022 [15]

3.1 Let's Avoid Knowledge Representation!

The knowledge representation problem in AI is the challenge of how to
formally represent knowledge in a way that a computer can understand
and reason about. This typically involves creating a set of symbols, rules,
and structures that can be used to represent concepts, relationships, and
other types of information. The goal is to create a representation that is

both expressive enough to capture all relevant aspects of the domain, and computationally tractable enough to allow for efficient reasoning and inference. There are many different approaches to knowledge representation, including logic-based, semantic networks, frames, and ontologies, each with their own strengths and weaknesses.

Deep learning techniques handle knowledge representation differently than traditional symbolic AI methods. Unlike symbolic AI which relies on explicit and hand-coded representations of knowledge, deep learning techniques learn to represent knowledge implicitly through the use of neural networks.

In deep learning, knowledge is represented in the form of the weights of the neural network. These weights are learned through training on a large dataset and they capture the underlying relationships and patterns in the data. The neural network can then use these learned weights to make predictions, classifications, or generate new data.

Deep learning models can handle large and complex datasets, and can automatically extract features from the data without the need for manual feature engineering. This makes them particularly well-suited for tasks such as image and speech recognition, natural language processing, and other areas where large amounts of data are available. However, they are not as good at explicating how they arrived at a decision, which can be a disadvantage.

In summary, deep learning techniques handle knowledge representation by learning the underlying patterns and relationships in the data through the use of neural networks, which can then be used for prediction, classification, and generation tasks. In GOFAI, knowledge is held by the programmer and explicitly coded into rules, while deep learning methods instead use data to guess the best rules from the relationships present in the dataset.

3.2 A Simple Neural Network is also a Linear Regression

A neural network can be mathematically equivalent to a regression or a decision tree under certain conditions.

A neural network is a machine learning model composed of layers of interconnected artificial neurons, which are designed to process and analyze data. They can be used for a wide range of tasks, such as image and speech recognition, natural language processing, and prediction.

A regression is a statistical method used to predict a continuous variable based on one or more input features. A linear regression, for example, is a simple neural network with one input layer, one output layer, and no hidden layers. In this case, the weights of the network are the coefficients of the linear equation and the network is equivalent to a linear regression model.

A decision tree is a tree-based model used for classification and prediction tasks. It consists of a series of if-then rules that are used to make decisions based on the input data. A neural network with one input layer, one output layer, and one hidden layer is equivalent to a decision tree. The network implements a piecewise linear function which can represent the decision boundaries of a decision tree. So, under certain conditions, a neural network can be mathematically equivalent to a linear regression or a decision tree. These conditions include having one input and one output layers, and having a specific activation function in the case of a decision tree [16].

3.3 Dummy Variables for Dummies (Wonkish)

Chapter Summary: It's all numbers, man. Machine learning techniques require that we turn everything (images, text, sound) into numbers and shove them into the model in the same way we use dummy variables in a simple regression. If you are satisfied with this, please skip this section. If you would like to learn a bit about the details and see some code examples, please keep reading. This section is necessarily technical, but should be approachable for anyone who has taken a college statistics class.

Dummy variables are used in regression analysis to include categorical variables in a model. Categorical variables are variables that take on a finite number of distinct values, such as "red", "green", "blue", "yes", or "no". Since these variables cannot be directly included in a regression model as they are not numerical, they need to be transformed into numerical variables.

The process of creating dummy variables is also known as one-hot encoding. It involves creating a new binary variable for each category of the original variable. For example, if you have a categorical variable "color" with three categories: "red", "green", "blue", you would create three binary variables: "color_red", "color_green", "color_blue". Each binary variable would take a value of 1 if the original variable is equal to the category; otherwise, it would be a value of 0.

When using dummy variables in a regression, it is important to remember to include only n-1 binary variables where n is the number of categories in the original variable. This is because including all n binary variables would result in perfect multicollinearity, which is when two or more independent variables are perfectly correlated. One of the binary variables can be dropped to avoid this problem.

Dummy variables are used in regression analysis to include categorical variables in a model. The process of creating dummy variables involves creating a new binary variable for each category of the original variable and one-hot encoding it. It is important to remember to include only n-1 binary variables to avoid perfect multicollinearity.

The creation of dummy variables in a regression is analogous to preprocessing image, text, and other data for a neural network for deep learning. This preprocessing is important as it ensures that the data is in a format that can be easily understood and processed by the network. The preprocessing steps for numbers, text, and images are slightly different.

For numbers:

▶ Normalization: It is common to normalize the input data by scaling it to have a mean of 0 and a standard deviation of 1. This helps to ensure that all input features have similar scales and prevents any one feature from dominating the network's computations.

▶ Imputation: Handling missing data is important, as it can negatively impact the model's performance. Common imputation techniques include replacing missing values with the mean, median, or mode of the feature.

For text:

▶ Tokenization: Text data must first be converted into a numerical format that can be understood by the network. This is typically done by tokenizing the text into individual words or n-grams and then encoding them as integers or real-valued vectors. A one-hot encoding exactly like the dummy variable method used in regression is also frequently used.

▶ Stop-words removal: The most common words in any language like "a", "an", "the", etc. that do not contain much meaning are called stop-words, they are often removed to reduce the dimensionality of the data.

▶ Stemming/Lemmatization: Words that have the same meaning can be stemmed or lemmatized to reduce the vocabulary size and increase the chances of generalization.

▶ Vocabulary Size: Each model must choose a vocabulary size or the maximum number of tokens that it will analyze. This may cause misspellings, slang or typos to be discarded in analysis.

For images:

▶ Converting to RGB or Greyscale: Each image is analyzed by its pixel color value, every point on an image will either have 3 color values (red, green, blue) or one single value (on a white/black scale) if the image is analyzed in greyscale.

▶ Convolutions: Pixel values are analyzed in groups that are defined by the model, since individual pixel values are only colors (or greyness) they must be combined together by the model to detect patterns like faces and stop signs. The method of convolution is defined by the model itself.

▶ Resizing: neural network can only accept images of a fixed size, so resizing the image to match the network's requirements is important.

▶ Normalization: It is common to normalize the pixel values to be in the range of 0-1 or -1 to 1. This will help the model converge faster.

▶ Data Augmentation: To increase the amount of data and prevent overfitting, common data augmentation techniques such as flipping, rotation, and cropping can be applied to the images.

In summary, preprocessing is an important step in training a neural network as it ensures that the data is in a format that can be easily understood and processed by the network. The preprocessing steps for numbers, text, and images involve normalization, imputation, tokenization, stop-words removal, stemming/lemmatization, resizing, and data augmentation.

3.4   Try That Again With A Few Billion Parameters

In the first section of this chapter, we introduced the idea that a simple neural network is mathematically equivalent to a regression. This is true and a useful way to think about neural networks and deep learning. In practice, a neural network trained on a gaming PC from 2023 can easily have millions of trainable parameters. A simple image classifier used to classify handwritten digits might have 60,000 parameters, which is about the number that was used in the model used by Yann LeCun and company in the 1990s. Bleeding-edge deep neural networks are trained on large GPU farms and have billions of trainable parameters. More parameters gives the models tremendous power to recognize complex patterns, but it also makes any practical attempt at explaining their inner-workings impossible.

When a neural network has a million (or more) trainable parameters and deep layers of neurons, it can be difficult to explain to a human what each of those parameters represents or how they contribute to the overall function of the network. This is because the interactions between the different layers and neurons can be complex and nonlinear, thereby making it challenging to understand the specific role of each parameter. The parameters model's complex interactions between the inputs makes it difficult to understand their specific function. Furthermore, in deep neural networks, the high number of layers can lead to a high level of abstraction, meaning that the individual neurons and their weights have little interpretability.

When a neural network has many interacting parameters, it can lead to mathematical chaos, which is a phenomenon where small changes in the initial conditions of the network can lead to vastly different outputs. This is because the interactions between the large number of parameters can create non-linear relationships that are sensitive to small changes. This can make it difficult to predict the behavior of the network, as small changes in the input or the parameters can lead to unexpected and seemingly random outputs.

3.5 Multicolinearity and the End of Science

Data science is a horrible term because it implies that data scientists are scientists and that the work they do is scientific, when in reality data scientists are not scientists and the work they do is not scientific. Data scientists use mathematics, statistics, and computer science to analyze data, but it is not scientific in the traditional sense. Data scientists do not use the scientific method and do not conduct experiments or develop theories. Data science is more akin to engineering or data analytics than actual scientific research.

The main goal of a scientist is to gain knowledge and understanding of the natural world through research, experimentation, and data analysis. Scientists make models of the world to test and explain. So-called data scientists make models too, but a model with layers of interacting parameters trained under chaotic conditions is almost impossible to explain. Multicollinearity is just one issue, but deep learning techniques are practically incompatible with the scientific method. With deep learning methods, it can be difficult to determine which variable had the most impact on the outcome of the model. Coefficients of the model can be unstable and unreliable, which can make it difficult to explain the model in a meaningful way.

Explaining the inner-workings of a neural network with millions of interacting parameters is difficult for many reasons. Most of the complexity is due to the number of parameters, which can make it difficult to understand how the model works and why it makes certain decisions. The interactions between the parameters are often non-linear and can be difficult to understand as the model can be sensitive to small changes in the parameters, which is the definition of mathematical chaos. This can make it difficult to explain why the model is making certain decisions as the interactions between the parameters are not always clear.

3.6 Let's Test Some Random Inputs! Feature Importance and Explainability

With a huge complex system of neurons that combine inputs in novel ways, it becomes very hard to understand which inputs are the most important for the system as a whole. To better understand deep learning models, data scientists use randomized or averaged inputs to a model to test the feature importance of a deep learning neural network. This type of testing is done to determine which features are most influential in the overall output of the network. This is done by randomly or averaging the input values for each feature and then running the model to see how the output is affected. For example, if a neural network is used to detect objects in an image, the data scientist may randomize the color of the objects to see how the model's accuracy is affected. If the accuracy drops significantly, they can infer that color is an important feature in the network.

Randomized or averaged inputs to a model can also be used to determine if a particular feature is necessary for the network to function correctly. For example, if the output of the network is not as accurate when a particular feature is randomized or averaged, then the data scientist can infer that this feature is important for the network's performance. By using this method, data scientists can gain insights into which features are important and which can be removed from the model to improve performance.

3.7 The Universal Machine Learning Workflow

The Universal Machine Learning Workflow is an important chapter in a technical guide for data scientists by the co-author of Tensorflow, the most popular machine learning framework in the world as of 2023, that outlines the *Universal* workflow for machine learning projects. I think this chapter should be understood by everyone using, investing in, and creating machine learning models.

Before Chollet gets into the details of model building, he chooses to begin with a note on ethics:

"You may sometimes be offered ethically dubious projects, such as "building an AI that rates the trustworthiness of someone from a picture of their face." First of all, the validity of the project is in doubt: it isn't clear why trustworthiness would be reflected on someone's face. Second, such a task opens the door to all kinds of ethical problems. Collecting a dataset for this task would amount to recording the biases and prejudices of the people who label the pictures. The models you would train on such data would merely encode these same biases into a black-box algorithm that would give them a thin veneer of legitimacy. In a largely tech-illiterate society like ours, "the AI algorithm said this person cannot be trusted" strangely appears to carry more weight and objectivity than "John Smith said this person cannot be trusted," despite the former being a learned approximation of the latter. Your model would be laundering and operationalizing at scale the worst aspects of human judgement, with negative effects on the lives of real people. [17]

Technology is never neutral. If your work has any impact on the world, this impact has a moral direction: technical choices are also ethical choices. Always be deliberate about the values you want your work to support."[17]

Chollet uses the outline below to explain the *Universal* workflow. I'll summarize the workflow and my own notes for a nontechnical audience here:

1. Define the Task
    a) Collect a Dataset
    b) Understand Your Data
    c) Choose a Measure of Success

2. Develop a Model
    a) Prepare the Data
    b) Choose an Evaluation Protocol
    c) Beat a Baseline
    d) Develop a model that overfits
    e) Regularize and Tune Your Model

3. Deploy the Model
   a) Explain Your Work to Your Stakeholders and Set Expectations
   b) Ship an Inference Model
   c) Monitor Your Model in the Wild
   d) Maintain Your Model

Of all of the steps in the workflow, "Defining The Task" and "Explaining The Work To Shareholders and Setting Expectations" are where the most miscommunication occurs.

In defining the task, machine learning engineers are often given impossible problems to solve, and because they want to keep paying their mortgage, they solve another related problem instead and allow stakeholders to jump to their own conclusions. By clearly understanding what a model is predicting and how the data is collected, some of this misunderstanding can be avoided.

I will discuss Large Language Models later, but they all do the same thing. They predict the next words in a sentence, just like the keyboard on your iPhone. They come up with amazing text, but by fundamentally understanding what they are predicting, you gain insight into their limitations. They are also all trained on the text publicly available on the internet; this includes scientific sources, but also fan-fiction and anime, so the idea that a model trained on this data could be relied on to predict anything truthful is preposterous.

Many models work like magic and many users assume models are predicting the future, when they are really correlating based on their past data. Even simple models of creditworthiness might have a similar problem. While building a creditworthiness model for a bank, due to lack of data, a machine learning engineer might (on purpose or inadvertently) create a model that predicts whether someone is a smoker instead of whether they are creditworthy. Because smoking and poverty are correlated, maybe the model "works", but it doesn't do what stakeholders think it does.

Setting expectations is another hellscape of misaligned incentives. Good machine learning engineers and data scientists are supposed to educate and advise stakeholders about the limitations of their own models. Read Chollet's advice on this topic below:

The expectations of non-specialists towards AI systems are often unrealistic. For example, they might expect that the system "understands" its task and is capable of exercising human-like common sense in the context of the task. To address this, you should consider showing some examples of the failure modes of your model (for instance, show what incorrectly classified samples look like, especially those for which the misclassification seems surprising).

They might also expect human-level performance, especially for processes that were previously handled by people. Most machine learning models, because they are (imperfectly) trained to approximate human-generated labels, do not nearly get there. You should clearly convey model performance expectations. Avoid using abstract statements like "The model has 98 percent accuracy" (which most people mentally round up to 100 percent), and prefer talking, for instance, about false negative rates and false positive rates. You could say, "With these settings, the fraud detection model would have a 5 percent false negative rate and a 2.5 percent false positive rate. Every day, an average of 200 valid transactions would be flagged as fraudulent and sent for manual review, and an average of 14 fraudulent transactions would be missed. An average of 266 fraudulent transactions would be correctly caught." Clearly relate the model's performance metrics to business goals.

You should also make sure to discuss with stakeholders the choice of key launch parameters- for instance, the probability threshold at which a transaction should be flagged (different thresholds will produce different false negative and false positive rates). Such decisions involve trade-offs that can only be handled with a deep understanding of the business context.[17]

One does not need to be a psychologist to understand that these conversations almost never happen. The workflow of machine learning is universal; we are all doing fancy regressions and we all deal with the same wild expectations, bad data and misalignment with business.

3.8 A Machine Learning Engineer is a Data Janitor

Since the machine learning workflow is *universal*, it is fairly straightforward to automate. There are a plethora of offerings from companies big and small who offer AutoML tools that anyone with basic Excel skills can use. Since modern AI is "all a regression", these tools do the regression for you. Users just need to feed them the data and the AutoML tool finds out the relationship. On the surface, it seems like the job of the machine learning engineer has become obsolete before it even became a proper discipline.

Despite the existence of AutoML tools, machine learning engineers (and data scientists) do some actual work. A 2016 CrowdFlower survey of 16,000 data scientists showed that on average we spend our time doing the following:

▶ **60 percent of a machine learning engineer's time is spent cleaning and organizing data** - we are data janitors! If you had great data ready in an Excel file, you would have been able to fit your own model without us. We need to organize the mess of data that exists in the world so it is in a nice format to fit in a model. For example, it is well known that almost all large language models use the same common crawl dataset (https://commoncrawl.org/), but how it is organized and weighted can change the quality of the outputs dramatically. The organization of the same dataset can lead to the same dataset either producing a nice predictive keyboard or something approaching ChatGPT.

▶ **19 percent of a machine learning engineer's time is spent collecting data.** We often start making models without a huge dataset, so data needs to be collected in order to make the first model, and after that first model (to match people for our new dating app, let's say) is deployed, we rely on users to provide us with data for future models. Collecting new data is a creative endeavor sometimes, and often involves human effort. Amazon's Mechanical Turk service has been leveraged for this purpose for years, and OpenAI has successfully deployed outsourced talent to solve some of the trickiest problems facing large language models.

▶ **9 percent of a machine learning engineer's time is spent fitting models.** We need to fit models; there is some art to choosing the right architecture and modeling techniques. An AutoML tool can do this reasonably well, too, but considering some fancy training servers cost $28 per hour or more, sometimes it is useful to have an expert guess the best model architecture and save time in training, even if that expert is getting paid $249,000 per year.

▶ **4 percent of a machine learning engineer's time is spent refining algorithms.** Many machine learning engineers spend almost no time doing this. Other researchers (corporate-academic types who write scientific papers) spend a lot of time doing this. It averages out to four percent but doesn't represent the average day of a machine learning engineer.

Overall, the main job of most machine learning engineers is to clean up and collect a ton of data, and then feed that data into the same machine learning model that everyone else is using; and then rinse and repeat.

3.9 Key Takeaways

▶ **Deep learning models are fundamentally large unscientific regressions.** They are trained to create a function that maps input data to output data.

▶ **Deep learning models are chaotic systems containing millions of interacting parameters.** They are not designed to be explained or created in such a way that their weights can be used for scientific analysis. They find reasonable answers and don't care how they get there. Multicollinearity (understanding the relationship of an input and output) and feature importance (understanding which inputs are most important) are only understandable with a high level of statistical error.

▶ **Small changes in inputs of a deep learning model may dramatically change the outputs.** Deep learning models are complex deterministic systems that can exhibit chaotic behavior. Their inner workings are functionally unknowable and practically impossible to test.

▶ **Machine learning engineers spend most of their time collecting and organizing data.** Because deep learning models often share common architecture, getting good data to train with is the best thing that an engineer can do to train good models. In practice, only a handful of corporate-academic types are experimenting with new and exciting architectures.

▶ **Deep learning models can have impressive and useful outputs, but the creators of models should be encouraged to highlight their failures and limitations.** Machine learning engineers might be more keen to highlight failures and limitations if they are encouraged to do so by their users, managers, and investors.

4

CREATIVITY AND DECISION MAKING WITH DEEP LEARNING MODELS

"AI Policy

I expect you to use AI (ChatGPT and image generation tools, at a minimum), in this class. In fact, some assignments will require it. Learning to use AI is an emerging skill, and I provide tutorials in Canvas about how to use them. I am happy to meet and help with these tools during office hours or after class

Beware of the limits of ChatGPT:

- *If you provide minimum effort prompts, you will get low quality results. You will need to refine you prompts to get good outcomes. This will take work.*

- *Don't trust anything it says. If it gives you a number or a fact, assume it is wrong unless you either know the answer or can check in with another source. You will be responsible for any errors or omissions provided by the tool. It works best for topics you understand.*

- *AI is a tool, but one that you need to acknowledge using. Please include a paragraph at the end of any assignment that uses AI explaining what you used the AI for and what prompts you used to get the results. Failure to do so is in violation of academic honesty policies*

▶ *Be thoughtful about when this tool is useful. Don't use it if it isn't appropriate for the case or circumstance."*

Dr. Ethan Mollick, 2023 - Syllabus for class at The Wharton School at the University of Pennsylvania

4.1   Theories of Creativity

Machine learning models use data (from the past) to discover rules and make classifications. Because of the way they are constructed, these classifications, suggestions, and artworks are by definition derivative or "having parts that originate from another source." I won't get into a philosophical discussion on what the nature of creativity is, but it's worth considering how using deep learning models biases us toward the past, but also could give us insights from other domains.

It can be argued that creativity is simply the combination of existing works. This is because many new ideas and innovations are often inspired by and built upon existing concepts. For example, a new form of music may be created by combining elements from different genres. Similarly, a new technology may be created by combining and improving upon existing technologies.

It can also be argued that creativity involves much more than just combining existing works. Creativity is not just about recombining existing ideas, but also about coming up with completely new and original concepts. This requires a unique perspective and a deep understanding of the subject matter as well as the ability to think outside the box.

Deep learning models of speech, when heavily used, may slow down the evolution of language. AI art models may slow down "progress" in art, whatever that means. Deep learning models of disease trained on data from

1980 may be irrelevant to today's diseases. That said, these same models may give us interesting insights in new domains; models trained on beautiful paintings may be put to use in a new domain (like designing beautiful interiors), and that model could give new insight to interior designers. Models of the interaction of ants could be put to use in designing cities, and so on and so forth. AI cuts many ways; it makes us faster but makes us more reliant on the past. Models can be used across domains but should be used intentionally and transparently when possible. Each use opens up a new world of possibilities for users, and sometimes a new headache for intellectual property lawyers. We'll discuss all of these topics in this chapter.

4.2   Creative Uses of Power Tools

Power tools, even simple ones like a drill, are complex machines that take human input and transform it using static rules. The pressure the user of a drill puts on the bit and the speed at which they pull the trigger all deterministically affect the output. Just because a tool is a deterministic machine doesn't mean it is unable to produce creative works.

What is happening as we use generative tools like ChatGPT or image-to-text models is that the "creative act" has been relocated. The creative act is now the prompt you give the tool, the users input. And someone can still be good at using AI, just like someone can be good at using any piece of software.

Modern AI is a complex system of algorithms, data, and analytics that can be used to solve complex problems. AI systems can learn from data, identify patterns, and make predictions about the future. AI systems are typically used to automate and assist human decision making. AI systems are programmed with specific objectives and goals, and the user input decides the output. For example, an AI system could be programmed to solve a mathematical problem and the user input would determine the parameters of the problem and the output would be the solution.

A power drill is also a complex deterministic system. The user input is limited to the type of drill bit, the speed of the drill, and the direction of the drill. The output is determined by these inputs as the drill will only drill in the direction and speed determined by the user. The user also has to choose the correct drill bit to ensure the drill can do the job correctly and safely.

Both modern deep learning models and a power drill are complex but ultimately deterministic systems. The user input, however limited it may be, ultimately controls the output of the system. Both systems require a user to understand how to use them and to make the correct input to get the desired output.

4.3   Garbage In, Garbage Out

The "Power Tool" of AI is a deterministic, static, and unchanging system; and the rules of that system are determined by the data that the model is shown. If a model is trained on bad data, it will produce poor results. End of story...

... maybe not. It's worth thinking about this for a moment. It is often said that modern AI can "generalize and make informed inferences given new data." If deep learning models are really just a big regression, these models will always come up with an answer; but if the world changes, these models will still be projecting complicated averages of their past data into the future.

So, let's separate AI's decision making into two extremes: *Creative Decision Making* and *Critical Decision Making*. The stakes are very low in a world of *Creative Decision Making*, and who cares if the AI is all a regression and it just mushes together the limited data that it's seen. In a creative context you can also ask an AI interesting questions, so long as you don't solely rely on it's output without checking the facts first. Even if "Garbage In, Garbage Out" holds, garbage can still be helpful for a creative process.

4.4   Garbage In, New Perspective Out?

For creative tasks, it generally doesn't matter that a deep learning model is unscientific or trained on a lopsided dataset. An informed user of AI knows this and can account for that in their decision making, especially when engaging in creative decision making. The situation becomes problematic once we allow deep learning models to engage in critical decision making by themselves.

Generative models will come up with amazing (but derivative) works of art, but they will never "change the game". A model of sculpture trained on past sculptures in 1917 will never come up with Marcel Duchamp's "Fountain". There is a term that machine learning engineers use for this when the rules of the game are changed; it's called "Concept Drift".

4.5   Concept Drift and the End of Usefulness

Concept drift refers to the phenomenon where the distribution of data changes over time, thereby causing the performance of deep learning models built on historical data to degrade. The model becomes less useful because it is trained to make predictions based on the relationship between the inputs and outputs in the data it was trained on, and if this relationship changes, the model may start making incorrect predictions. This is particularly problematic in real-world applications where the data is constantly evolving and the relationship between inputs and outputs is subject to change. To mitigate the effects of concept drift, it is often necessary to continually retrain deep learning models on updated data.

The frequency with which a deep learning model needs to be retrained to mitigate the effects of concept drift depends on several factors, including the rate at which the data distribution changes, the size and complexity of the model, and the availability of computational resources.

For some applications with relatively stable data distributions, retraining the model once every few months or even once per year may be sufficient.

However, in other applications where the data is changing rapidly, it may be necessary to retrain the model more frequently, such as once per week or even once per day.

Ultimately, the frequency of retraining will depend on the specific requirements of the application, and the trade- off between the cost of retraining and the potential cost of incorrect predictions. In general, it's recommended to monitor the performance of the model over time and to retrain it as needed to ensure that it remains accurate and relevant.

If a deployed deep learning model is not monitored, there are several risks that can emerge:

- Accuracy degradation: As the data distribution changes over time, the model may become less accurate, leading to incorrect predictions. This can result in financial losses, reduced customer satisfaction, or even harm to individuals.

- Bias amplification: deep learning models can be biased, and if this bias is not monitored and addressed, it can be amplified over time as the model continues to make incorrect predictions. This can result in discriminatory outcomes, such as unequal treatment of individuals based on protected characteristics such as race, gender, or age.

- Legal liability: In some cases, incorrect predictions made by deep learning models can result in legal liability, particularly if the model is being used to make decisions that have significant consequences, such as in the criminal justice system or in medical diagnosis.

- Reputational damage: If a deep learning model is making incorrect predictions, it can damage the reputation of the organization deploying the model, potentially leading to a loss of customers or investors.

It is important to monitor deep learning models once they are deployed, and to take action to address any issues that arise, such as retraining the model or adjusting its parameters, in order to mitigate these risks and ensure that the model continues to perform well over time.

4.6 The Impossibility of Fairness

Achieving fairness in deep learning models can be challenging, and to some extent it may be impossible to completely eliminate all forms of bias. This is because deep learning models are trained on historical data, which may contain biases and disparities that are perpetuated in the model's predictions. One can attempt to "fix the training set", but in practice, models will continue to bias their prediction to past data or their creators' careful curation of the past. [18]

However, it is possible to reduce the impact of bias in deep learning models through careful design and monitoring of the model's performance. This may include techniques such as fairness constraints, algorithmic transparency, and regular auditing of the model's predictions to identify and address any issues of bias.

It's important to note that fairness is a complex and multi-faceted concept, and different definitions of fairness may be appropriate for different applications. For example, some definitions of fairness may prioritize equal treatment of all individuals, while others may prioritize proportional representation or equal opportunities.

Ultimately, the extent to which fairness is achievable in deep learning models will depend on the specific requirements of the application and the level of effort that is put into designing and monitoring the model to ensure that it is making fair and unbiased predictions.

4.7 Transfer Learning Everywhere

Transfer learning is a machine learning technique that involves transferring knowledge from one model trained on a task to another model trained on a related task. The idea behind transfer learning is that a model that has been trained on one task can be fine-tuned for another task, reducing the amount of labeled data required to train the new model.

For example, imagine that you have a deep learning model that has been trained to recognize objects in natural images (e.g., cats, dogs, balls, cars). You can use the knowledge learned by this model as a starting point to train a new model that recognizes objects in medical images, such as X-rays or MRI scans. The new model can start with the weights of the pre-trained model and fine-tune them on the new task, using a much smaller amount of labeled data than would be required to train the model from scratch.

Transfer learning can be useful in many different applications, particularly when labeled data is scarce or expensive to obtain. By leveraging knowledge from a pre-trained model, transfer learning can help to improve the performance of new models, reduce the amount of data required for training, and accelerate the development of new machine learning applications.

I asked ChatGPT to "tell me a story of transfer learning going horribly wrong in the context of online dating, with a model trained in the Middle East being deployed by an American dating app," and here's what it said:

> *"Once upon a time, an American online dating company decided to use transfer learning to improve their matchmaking algorithms. They trained a state-of-the-art machine learning model on a large dataset of profiles and dating preferences from the Middle East. The model was able to suggest matches with remarkable accuracy and the company was confident that it would perform just as well in the American market.*
>
> *However, things went terribly wrong when they deployed the model on their American dating app. The model was not properly trained to consider the cultural and social differences between the Middle East*

and America. As a result, it suggested matches that were inappropriate and offensive, causing widespread backlash and criticism from users.

For example, the model suggested matches between people of different religious backgrounds, which was not acceptable to many users. It also suggested matches between people with significant age gaps, which was not socially acceptable in the American market.

The company was forced to remove the model and start from scratch, causing significant harm to their reputation and financial losses. They learned the hard way that transfer learning can only be effective if the model is properly trained on relevant and culturally appropriate data.

This story serves as a cautionary tale about the importance of considering cultural differences and ethical implications when deploying machine learning models in different regions and markets."

Not bad I think... picking good training data and doing good "data janitoring" is the main job of a machine learning engineer. If the past is not like the future, you are also doing transfer learning. Most models steal data from other sources; so are doing transfer learning, too. This is fine, but do we know that we are doing this? A model that is deployed in a domain experiencing concept drift and continues to make predictions without being retrained can be considered to be doing a harmful form of transfer learning. This is because the model has been trained on a different distribution of data (the past), and is being applied to a new domain with a different distribution (the present and future). In traditional transfer learning, the goal is to transfer knowledge from one domain to another related domain where the data distributions are similar enough to enable the model to make accurate predictions. However, in the case of concept drift, the data distributions are changing over time, and the model is becoming less accurate as a result.

By continuing to make predictions without being retrained, the model is essentially "transferring" its knowledge from a historical data distribution to a new, changed data distribution, which may not be a valid assumption. This can result in incorrect predictions and other negative outcomes, such as harm to individuals or organizations.

4.8 Industrial-Scale Plagiarism

Aside from regurgitating the past and predictions from other domains, deep learning models can also enable plagiarism on an industrial scale. Early text generation models could be made to write entire sections of *Harry Potter* when fed the opening lines of a chapter. Even as models grow large and with more sophisticated users, researchers, and lawyers, they are still able to "extract the training data" from large models[19], causing headaches for their creators and adding to the work of intellectual property lawyers.

To avoid this creators of deep learning models have the following tools at their disposal:

- Best practices in machine learning: data preprocessing, augmentation, regularization, model architecture choices, early stopping, and validation are all things that we are taught to do to prevent overfitting.

- Contractual agreements: Microsoft (owner of github and cocreator of the Github Copilot code generation model) has a special contract for anyone submitting code to github that essentially says that "we are allowed to use this code to train our models, and if our models regenerate your copyrighted code, you can kick rocks."

- Release the Kraken: StabilityAI's Stable Diffusion model was released as open source software, they still managed to get sued[20], but they basically said, "this model was trained on all copyrighted and copylefted images on the web, sometimes it'll generate stuff that violates copyright law, but we are in Germany and will give this thing away for free to the public, and see how Getty Images, photographers and graphic designers of the world handle it... good luck!".

These techniques can help to reduce the risk of having deep learning models reproduce the training data and cause intellectual property disputes, but there is no way to completely eliminate these risks, they are simply side-effects of the method of machine learning that we are doing nowadays. If you are an IP lawyer and need an expert witness, I'm your man: brad@bradflaugher.com.

4.9 Working Together is Best

It turns out sometimes that the best combination is a reasonably smart (but not too cocky) human who gets recommendations from a few deep learning models.

Garry Kasparov, the legendary chess player we heard about in chapter 1, witnessed a tournament where humans and AI could compete together. The tournament was designed to showcase the strengths of both humans and AI, and how they could work together to achieve incredible results here is what Garry says about the tournament:

> *"Once again, the chess world offers a useful test case for how this collaboration can play out. In 2005 the online chess playing site Playchess.com hosted what it called a "freestyle" chess tournament in which anyone could compete in teams with other players or computers. What made this competition interesting is that several groups of grandmasters working with computers also participated in this tournament. Predictably, most people expected that one of these grandmasters in combination with a supercomputer would dominate this competition ; but that's not what happened. The tournament was won by a pair of amateur American chess players using three computers. It was their ability to coordinate and coach effectively their computers that defeated the combination of a smart grandmaster and a PC with great computational power."*[21]

The tournament was a huge success, and showed that when humans and AI work together, they can achieve amazing things. The tournament participants learned that AI is not just a tool, but a valuable partner, and that by combining their strengths, they could achieve results that neither could have accomplished on their own. The tournament inspired many people to explore the potential of human-AI collaboration, and showed that by embracing technology, we can create a brighter future for all.

AI is an amazing partner, but we need to think for ourselves too. We can't blindly trust AI, but we can use it to inspire and challenge us.[22]

4.10 Key Takeaways

- **When you are using deep learning models, you are almost always engaging in some kind of transfer learning.** You are assuming the past will be like the future, or that training set reflects reality, which isn't always the case.

- **Models can puke out seemingly creative things, but they are still a product of their training data.** Deep learning models are deterministic systems, they slap together data based on rules they guessed from their training data. This process can still be very useful, but deep learning models are not sentient creative creatures from science fiction.

- **Even if you think you "own the rights" to the output of a model, models can sometimes puke out their training data.** Modelers try their best to prevent this but models can spit out their training data, which may cause headaches for everyone except the intellectual property lawyers.

- **Users should consider the quality and appropriateness of the data the model they are using is trained on before deciding to use a model.** Remember, machine learning engineers spend most of their time cleaning up and gathering data, if you ask questions about how and when the data was collected and cleaned up you can get ahead of potential problems of concept drift and blind transfer learning (engaging in transfer learning without your consent).

Work with the technology. Don't make your model do everything, sometimes it'll come up with stupid answers. Also don't assume you are always right, try and remember the story of the freestyle chess tournament and the grandmasters who got beat by the amateurs getting reasonable advice from a few chess engines. Working with your model, as if it were a coworker who you don't fully trust, but still think is smart is probably the best way to use deep learning models.

5

CASE STUDIES

5.1 Introduction

This chapter is a dissection of every important model I could think of, and many that I have built myself. If our goal is to understand and critique AI models, then we need to understand the models themselves. I know of no better way to understand than to take models apart then rebuild them. In the first four chapters you learned all of the key topics you need to do a high-level dissection (if you haven't read the first four chapters please go back and do that).

To facilitate this dissection I am going to use a tool called a **model card**. Model cards are a way to document the capabilities and limitations of your AI model. They are a useful tool for understanding your model, and for communicating its capabilities and limitations to others. Google (see https://modelcards.withgoogle.com/face-detection), Huggingface and even small makers of AI models produce model cards to help educate their users and developers, and as you can imagine no one reads them.

In this chapter I am going to create and add commentary to model cards for many popular models. Whether you are a technical person or not I want you to be able to read and understand these, and eventually I want my notes or criticisms to become self-evident. My idea is that once you understand the data that is used to train a model and the domain that it is deployed, you can forecast its strengths and weaknesses almost automatically. Let's try a few and see how it goes.

Note that I'll introduce these models in a very particular order. I'll also save the hairiest models (self-driving cars and autonomous weapons) their own chapters for a deeper discussion. Try and follow along in the order that I lay out here, but only until you get bored. Once you are bored and can forecast my criticisms, you can skip around with impunity.

I'm happy to add future dissections or model cards to this chapter, so if you have a favorite model that you'd like to see dissection of, please let me know by emailing: brad@bradflaugher.com.

5.1.1 *Sucker Traps to Note When Analyzing Models*

> *"The sucker's trap is when you focus on what you know*
> *and what others don't know, rather than the reverse."*
> *Nassim Taleb, 2016*[23]

In chapters 1-4 there were a number of key concepts that we discussed that I'll call "Sucker Traps". Below is a list of those concepts that I will refer to regularly when discussing the model cards in this chapter:

- Creative or Critical: The difference between a model that is used to inform a decision and a model that is used to make a decision.

- Explainability: The ability to understand why a model makes a particular prediction.

- Plagiarism: The capacity for a model to output copyrighted material from its training data.

- Concept Drift: The possibility and frequency of changes in the relationships in the training data.

▶ Editorializing: The possibility of a modeler either explicitly or accidentally creating a biased training set and thus permanently shifting the outputs of the model away from reality.

5.1.2 *Key Terms*

▶ **Accuracy:** The proportion of correctly classified examples to the total number of examples.

▶ **AUC:** Area under the Receiver Operating Characteristic (ROC) curve.

▶ **F1:** Harmonic mean of precision and recall.

▶ **False Negative (FN):** An instance that is actually positive but predicted as negative.

▶ **False Positive (FP):** An instance that is actually negative but predicted as positive.

▶ **Precision:** The proportion of correctly classified positive examples to the total number of positive examples predicted by the model.

▶ **Recall:** The proportion of correctly classified positive examples to the total number of actual positive examples.

▶ **True Negative (TN):** An instance that is actually negative and predicted as negative.

▶ **True Positive (TP):** An instance that is actually positive and predicted as positive.

5.2 Model Cards

5.2.1 *Fluid Dynamics*

- ▶ **Description:** This model is intended to predict fluid flow patterns in various applications, such as aerodynamics, hydrodynamics, and weather forecasting.

- ▶ **Training Data:** The model is trained on a large dataset of numerical simulations of fluid flow patterns, which includes various geometries, fluid properties, and boundary conditions. The data is generated using well-established simulation tools such as the finite element method, finite volume method, or lattice Boltzmann method.

- ▶ **Evaluation:** The model is evaluated on a separate dataset of numerical simulations of fluid flow patterns that are not seen during training. The evaluation dataset includes a variety of geometries, fluid properties, and boundary conditions. The model's performance is measured using common metrics in fluid dynamics such as root-mean-square error (RMSE), mean absolute error (MAE), and correlation coefficient (R).

- ▶ **Limits and Risks:** This model is intended for scientific and engineering applications and is not directly used for decision-making that affects human lives. However, the model's predictions may indirectly affect human lives by informing engineering design or emergency response planning. It is important to validate the model's accuracy and uncertainty, and to communicate the limitations and assumptions of the model to stakeholders. The model assumes that the fluid flow is governed by the Navier-Stokes equations, which may not be accurate for highly turbulent or rarefied flows. The model may also be limited by the numerical precision and stability of the simulation tools used to generate the training data.

▶ **Common Myths or Misunderstandings:** Models of physical processes are excellent ways to experiment with the world as it is understood. However, if this model is trained on data that is not representative, it will lead its users to draw incorrect conclusions about the fluids that are being studied. This tool also should not be used by itself, think of this tool like the wind tunnels used to test the aerodynamics of a car. You probably want to road test the car as well, but if you can use a model to decrease the cost of your experimentation (by disqualifying models before they get to the road-test phase) then please do it. Said differently, don't let this model make any critical decisions, but let it participate in the creative process.

▶ **Quality Grade:** B+

▶ **Cost to Create:** $100,000

▶ **Creator's Note:** This model is probably not too difficult to copy if its training data is easy to gather. It would be difficult to detect whether someone used this model to create their product considering how stable the laws of physics are and how good this model should perform.

5.2.2 *Shakespearean Text*

▶ **Description:** The Shakespearean Text Generator is a type of language model that's specifically designed to generate text in the style of William Shakespeare. It's based on deep learning algorithms, such as the Transformer architecture, and is trained on a large corpus of Shakespearean text. The model uses this training data to learn patterns and structures in Shakespeare's writing, and can then generate new text that mimics the style and language of the Bard himself.

▶ **Training Data:** The Shakespearean Text Generator is trained on a large corpus of text written by William Shakespeare. This can include plays, sonnets, and other works by the Bard. The quality and quantity of the training data will impact the performance of the model, so it's important to use a high-quality corpus that accurately represents Shakespeare's writing.

▶ **Evaluation:** The performance of the Shakespearean Text Generator can be evaluated using a variety of metrics, such as perplexity, BLEU score, or human evaluation. Human evaluation is particularly useful for language models like this one, as it allows experts in Shakespearean literature to assess the quality of the generated text and compare it to the real works of Shakespeare.

▶ **Use Cases:** The Shakespearean Text Generator has a number of potential use cases, including:
  1. Generating new Shakespearean-style plays or sonnets
  2. Analyzing Shakespeare's writing style and language
  3. Creating educational materials and games that teach students about Shakespeare and his works
  4. Providing inspiration for creative writing and poetry

▶ **Limits and Risks:** Like any language model, the Shakespearean Text Generator has limitations and risks. One of the main limitations is that it may not always generate text that is grammatically correct or semantically meaningful. Additionally, the model may struggle to capture all of the nuances and complexities of Shakespeare's writing, and may generate text that is not true to the style or spirit of the Bard.

▶ **Common Myths or Misunderstandings:** There are a few common myths or misunderstandings about the Shakespearean Text Generator. One myth is that the model can perfectly recreate Shakespeare's writing, when in reality it can only generate text that is similar in style. It's a great creative tool but that's about it. You'll also of course run into issues of plagiarism and model outputs should be checked to see their similarity to Shakespeare's actual work, compared to the whole internet, Shakespeare's corpus is very small and the model may have a tendency to output its training data in raw form.

▶ **Quality Grade:** A+

▶ **Cost to Create:** $10,000

▶ **Creator's Note:** Considering Shakesepeare's plays are in the public domain, this model is probably not too difficult to copy if its training data is easy to gather. Considering the unique style of Shakespeare's writing, it would be easy to detect whether someone used this model to create their product.

5.2.3 *Lithium Mining*

▶ **Description:** The Lithium Mining Site Classifier is a type of machine learning model that's designed to identify potential lithium mining sites based on a set of features. The model can be trained on a dataset of known lithium mining sites and their associated features, such as geology, topography, and geochemical data. The trained model can then be used to identify new potential mining sites by predicting the likelihood of a site containing lithium based on its feature set.

▶ **Training Data:** The Lithium Mining Site Classifier is trained on a dataset of known lithium mining sites and their associated features. This dataset should include a representative sample of mining sites, with a balanced distribution of positive (lithium-containing) and negative (non-lithium-containing) examples. The quality and quantity of the training data will impact the performance of the model, so it's important to use high-quality data that accurately represents the characteristics of lithium mining sites.

▶ **Evaluation:** The performance of the Lithium Mining Site Classifier can be evaluated using a variety of metrics, such as accuracy, precision, recall, and F1 score. These metrics can be used to compare different models and to track the progress of a model as it's trained on more data. Additionally, the model can be validated using independent test data that was not used during training, to assess its ability to generalize to new, unseen data.

▶ **Use Cases:** The Lithium Mining Site Classifier has a number of potential use cases, including:
1. Identifying new potential lithium mining sites
2. Prioritizing exploration efforts by ranking the likelihood of a site containing lithium
3. Supporting decision-making in the lithium mining industry by providing a quantitative assessment of the potential of a site

▶ **Limits and Risks:** Like any machine learning model, the Lithium Mining Site Classifier has limitations and risks. One of the main limitations is that it may not always be accurate, and may misclassify sites as either positive (lithium-containing) or negative (non-lithium-containing). Additionally, the model may be biased toward certain features if the training data is not representative of the true distribution of mining sites.

▶ **Common Myths or Misunderstandings:** There are a few common myths or misunderstandings about the Lithium Mining Site Classifier. One myth is that the model can always accurately identify lithium mining sites, when in reality it can only provide a prediction based on the information it was trained on. Another myth is that the model can replace the expertise of geologists and mining engineers, when in reality it is intended to support and enhance their decision-making processes. Don't expect this model to be able to explain itself though.

▶ **Quality Grade:** B

▶ **Cost to Create:** $250,000

▶ **Creator's Note:** Again, data collection is the difficult part here. For this model to be good one needs to collect good data, and that data is expensive which makes this model hard to copy.

5.2.4 *Chess*

▶ **Description:** The Chess Playing Model is a type of machine learning model that's designed to play the game of chess. It can be trained on a dataset of chess games and moves, and can then be used to make predictions about the best move to play in a given chess position. The model can be based on a variety of machine learning algorithms, including reinforcement learning, deep learning, or Monte Carlo tree search.

▶ **Training Data:** The Chess Playing Model is typically trained on a large dataset of chess games and moves, which can include both human and computer-generated games. The size and quality of the training data will impact the performance of the model, so it's important to use a diverse and representative dataset that accurately represents the game of chess.

▶ **Evaluation:** The performance of the Chess Playing Model can be evaluated using a variety of metrics, such as win rate, ELO rating, or human evaluation. These metrics can be used to compare different models and to track the progress of a model as it's trained on more data. Additionally, the model can be tested against human opponents or other chess-playing models to assess its ability to play the game effectively.

▶ **Use Cases:** The Chess Playing Model has a number of potential use cases, including:
1. Playing the game of chess against human or computer opponents
2. Analyzing chess games and moves to identify patterns and strategies
3. Supporting chess education and training by providing a challenging opponent for students and players
4. Developing new and innovative chess-related products and services

▶ **Limits and Risks:** Like any machine learning model, the Chess Playing Model has limitations and risks. One of the main limitations is that it may not always make the best move, and may make mistakes or suboptimal moves. Additionally, the model may be biased toward certain openings, strategies, or styles of play if the training data is not representative of the game of chess as a whole.

▶ **Common Myths or Misunderstandings:** There are a few common myths or misunderstandings about the Chess Playing Model. One myth is that the model can always beat human opponents, when in reality it can only make predictions based on the information it was trained on. Another myth is that the model can replace human expertise and creativity in the game of chess, when in reality it is intended to support and enhance human players' abilities.

▶ **Quality Grade:** A

▶ **Cost to Create:** $10,000

▶ **Creator's Note:** Good chess models are a dime a dozen these days, and the data is easy to collect (you can make up data yourself using reinforcement learning). You can also use output from other models to help train yours so this model is very easy to copy. As far as detection goes, the picture is less clear; if the model behaves significantly differently from a grandmaster, then it would be easy to detect, but if not you could use this model on the sly. Furthermore, this model could be trained to make "human" mistakes to avoid detection.

5.2.5 *Go*

▶ **Description:** The Go Playing Model is a type of machine learning model that's designed to play the game of Go. It can be trained on a dataset of Go games and moves, and can then be used to make predictions about the best move to play in a given Go position. The model can be based on a variety of machine learning algorithms, including reinforcement learning, deep learning, or Monte Carlo tree search.

▶ **Training Data:** The Go Playing Model is typically trained on a large dataset of Go games and moves, which can include both human and computer-generated games. The size and quality of the training data will impact the performance of the model, so it's important to use a diverse and representative dataset that accurately represents the game of Go.

▶ **Evaluation:** The performance of the Go Playing Model can be evaluated using a variety of metrics, such as win rate, ELO rating, or human evaluation. These metrics can be used to compare different models and to track the progress of a model as it's trained on more data. Additionally, the model can be tested against human opponents or other Go-playing models to assess its ability to play the game effectively.

▶ **Use Cases:** The Go Playing Model has a number of potential use cases, including:
   1. Playing the game of Go against human or computer opponents
   2. Analyzing Go games and moves to identify patterns and strategies
   3. Supporting Go education and training by providing a challenging opponent for students and players
   4. Developing new and innovative Go-related products and services

▶ **Limits and Risks:** Like any machine learning model, the Go Playing Model has limitations and risks. One of the main limitations is that it may not always make the best move, and may make mistakes or suboptimal moves. Additionally, the model may be biased toward certain openings, strategies, or styles of play if the training data is not representative of the game of Go as a whole.

▶ **Common Myths or Misunderstandings:** There are a few common myths or misunderstandings about the Go Playing Model. One myth is that the model can always beat human opponents, when in reality it can only make predictions based on the information it was trained on. If the game is played differently than the data it was trained on, the model is likely to fail. **This has happened in the past with seemingly "stupid" openings breaking world-class go playing models, it clearly illustrates the fragility of deep learning models in general, and their near total dependence on their training sets, as well as their lack of "knowledge" and "understanding" as commonly depicted**[24]. Another myth is that the model can replace human expertise and creativity in the game of Go, when in reality it is intended to support and enhance human players' abilities. Know and understand a the model's limitations before you use it.

▶ **Quality Grade:** A

▶ **Cost to Create:** $30,000

▶ **Creator's Note:** Go is a more difficult game than chess so this model is more difficult to create, that said it would not be too difficult to copy and detect.

5.2.6 Large Stock Order

▶ **Description:** The Large NYSE Stock Order Classifier is a type of machine learning model that's designed to classify large stock orders on the New York Stock Exchange (NYSE) as either "aggressive" or "passive". Aggressive orders are those that are intended to have a significant impact on the stock price, while passive orders are those that are intended to have a minimal impact. The model can be trained on a dataset of large stock orders and their associated features, such as order size, order type, and trading volume.

▶ **Training Data:** The Large NYSE Stock Order Classifier is trained on a dataset of large stock orders and their associated features. This dataset should include a representative sample of aggressive and passive orders, with a balanced distribution of both types of orders. The quality and quantity of the training data will impact the performance of the model, so it's important to use high-quality data that accurately represents the characteristics of large NYSE stock orders.

▶ **Evaluation:** The performance of the Large NYSE Stock Order Classifier can be evaluated using a variety of metrics, such as accuracy, precision, recall, and F1 score. These metrics can be used to compare different models and to track the progress of a model as it's trained on more data. Additionally, the model can be validated using independent test data that was not used during training, to assess its ability to generalize to new, unseen data.

▶ **Use Cases:** The Large NYSE Stock Order Classifier has a number of potential use cases, including:
 1. Identifying aggressive and passive large stock orders on the NYSE
 2. Supporting market surveillance and regulatory compliance by detecting potential market manipulation
 3. Providing insights into market behavior and trends by analyzing the characteristics of aggressive and passive large stock orders

4. Supporting algorithmic trading by classifying large stock orders in real-time

▶ **Limits and Risks:** Like any machine learning model, the Large NYSE Stock Order Classifier has limitations and risks. One of the main limitations is that it may not always be accurate, and may misclassify orders as either aggressive or passive. Additionally, the model may be biased toward certain features if the training data is not representative of the true distribution of large NYSE stock orders.

▶ **Common Myths or Misunderstandings:** There are a few common myths or misunderstandings about the Large NYSE Stock Order Classifier. One myth is that the model can always accurately classify aggressive and passive orders, when in reality it can only provide a prediction based on the information it was trained on. Another myth is that the model can replace human expertise and judgement in market surveillance and regulatory compliance, when in reality it is intended to support and enhance human decision-making processes. This might be a great performing model for a time, but consider that the players in the market change quite often, and you while you might create a model that detects trades coming from Warren Buffett (so you can copy him) but he might change his tactics, or other Buffett lookalikes might enter the market and confuse your model, concept drift is everywhere in the market.

▶ **Quality Grade:** B+

▶ **Cost to Create:** $100,000

▶ **Creator's Note:** This model is exactly as good as the data you give it. If you have a good dataset that accurately flags Warren Buffett's past orders, then you can make a good model to flag his future orders. If you have poor data, this model will not be great. Since this data is so difficult, it is hard to copy, and probably hard to detect that you are using it.

5.2.7 *Share Tender Purchase*

▶ **Description:** The Share Tender Purchase Model is a deep learning model used in finance to predict the likelihood of a company's shares being purchased through a tender offer. It uses historical data about the company and market conditions to make its predictions.

▶ **Training Data:** The model is trained on historical data from previous tender offer situations, including data on the company being targeted, the offer price, and market conditions at the time. It may also be trained on data related to the target company's financial performance and other relevant factors.

▶ **Evaluation:** The model's performance is typically evaluated using metrics such as accuracy, precision, and recall, by comparing its predictions to actual outcomes of past tender offer situations. Additionally, the model's usefulness may be evaluated in terms of its ability to inform investment decisions and generate profitable returns.

▶ **Use Cases:** The Share Tender Purchase Model is primarily used by investors and financial analysts to inform investment decisions related to companies targeted for tender offers. It can be used to identify potentially profitable investments, as well as to inform decisions about whether to participate in a tender offer or to hold shares in the target company.

▶ **Limits and Risks:** Like all models, the Share Tender Purchase Model is subject to limitations and risks. It may not perform well if market conditions change significantly from those observed in the training data, or if there are factors not included in the model that impact the outcome of tender offer situations. Additionally, reliance on the model's predictions may lead to missed opportunities or losses if the model's predictions are inaccurate.

▶ **Common Myths or Misunderstandings:** One common myth about the Share Tender Purchase Model is that it can accurately predict the outcome of all tender offer situations. In reality, the model is only as accurate as the quality of its training data and the factors included in the model. Additionally, the model's predictions may be impacted by unpredictable events or circumstances, such as changes in government regulations or unexpected market events. This is another area where it's best to understand and monitor for concept drift.

▶ **Quality Grade:** B+

▶ **Cost to Create:** $100,000

▶ **Creator's Note:** This model is also as good as the data you give it, if you have detailed data on past tender offers, you can make a good model. If you have poor data, this model will not be great. Since this data is so difficult it is hard to copy, and probably hard to detect that you are using it.

5.2.8 *Stock Trading*

▶ **Description:** The Stock Trading Bot is a type of machine learning model that's designed to trade stocks automatically. It can be trained on a dataset of stock market data and make predictions about future stock prices and trends. The model can then use these predictions to execute trades, buying and selling stocks based on its predictions. The model can be based on a variety of machine learning algorithms, including reinforcement learning, deep learning, or decision trees.

▶ **Training Data:** The Stock Trading Bot is typically trained on a large dataset of stock market data, including historical prices, trading volumes, and other relevant market indicators. The size and quality of the training data will impact the performance of the model, so it's important to use a diverse and representative dataset that accurately represents the stock market.

▶ **Evaluation:** The performance of the Stock Trading Bot can be evaluated using a variety of metrics, such as return on investment (ROI), Sharpe ratio, or draw down. These metrics can be used to compare different models and to track the performance of a model over time. Additionally, the model can be tested using historical data to assess its ability to generate profits in a simulated trading environment.

▶ **Use Cases:** The Stock Trading Bot has a number of potential use cases, including:
1. Automating stock trading decisions and executions
2. Generating profits through stock trading
3. Supporting investment and portfolio management by providing a quantitative assessment of stock market trends and predictions

▶ **Limits and Risks:** Like any machine learning model, the Stock Trading Bot has limitations and risks. One of the main limitations is that it may not always generate profits, and may make mistakes or suboptimal trades. Additionally, the model may be biased toward certain stocks, sectors, or market conditions if the training data is not representative of the stock market as a whole.

▶ **Common Myths or Misunderstandings:** There are a few common myths or misunderstandings about the Stock Trading Bot. One myth is that the model can always generate profits, when in reality it can only make predictions based on the information it was trained on and can be impacted by market conditions and other factors. This model should be understood as being the worst of the stock trading models mentioned, mostly because it is so poorly defined. What is it doing exactly? Explainability in a model with such a huge scope is a problem, but I also would argue the market changes every day, thereby causing concept drift to render this model useless very quickly, where the previous models (large order and tender offer) might last a few days, weeks or maybe months.

▶ **Quality Grade:** C

▶ **Cost to Create:** $1,000

▶ **Creator's Note:** Every student who takes my bootcamp starts off wanting to make this model. It is so poorly defined that it is very easy to copy, and if you only use public pricing data it is not very hard to make. It will not be accurate at all though, and generally give you unhelpful advice like "go back in time and buy AAPL". Thanks, model!

5.2.9 *Horse Racing*

▶ **Description:** The Horse Racing Prediction model is a type of machine learning model that predicts the outcome of horse races. It can be trained on a dataset of historical horse racing data, including horse and jockey statistics, track conditions, and other relevant factors that can influence race outcomes. The model can then use these predictions to generate betting recommendations or inform decisions about which horses to bet on.

▶ **Training Data:** The Horse Racing Prediction model is typically trained on a large dataset of historical horse racing data that includes information on horses, jockeys, tracks, and other relevant factors. The size and quality of the training data will impact the performance of the model, so it's important to use a diverse and representative dataset that accurately represents the horse racing industry.

▶ **Evaluation:** The performance of the Horse Racing Prediction model can be evaluated using metrics such as accuracy, precision, and recall. These metrics can be used to compare different models and to track the performance of a model over time. Additionally, the model can be tested using historical data to assess its ability to generate profits in a simulated betting environment.

▶ **Use Cases:** The Horse Racing Prediction model has a number of potential use cases, including:
1. Generating profits through betting on horse races
2. Supporting betting and gambling by providing a quantitative assessment of horse racing predictions
3. Supporting horse racing management by predicting the outcome of horse races and providing recommendations for horse and jockey selection

▶ **Limits and Risks:** Like any machine learning model, the Horse Racing Prediction model has limitations and risks. One of the main limitations is that it may not always generate profits and may make mistakes or suboptimal betting recommendations. Additionally, the model may be biased towards certain horses, jockeys, or racing conditions if the training data is not representative of the horse racing industry as a whole.

▶ **Common Myths or Misunderstandings:** One common misunderstanding is that the Horse Racing Prediction model can always generate profits, when in reality it can only make predictions based on the information it was trained on and can be impacted by various factors that may influence the outcome of horse races. Additionally, the model may be prone to over fitting if not properly validated on independent datasets.

▶ **Quality: Grade:** B

▶ **Cost to Create:** $100,000

▶ **Creator's Note:** The Horse Racing Prediction model can be a profitable tool for experienced horse racing bettors, but it requires careful training and validation to ensure accurate predictions. The cost to create this model may vary depending on the size and quality of the training data used, as well as the complexity of the machine learning algorithms used.

5.2.10 *Sperm Counter*

▶ **Description:** This AI model is designed to count sperm in a video of semen under a microscope.

▶ **Training Data:** The model was trained on a large dataset of semen videos taken under a microscope. The training data was annotated with the number of sperm in each video, allowing the model to learn the patterns and features of sperm in different types of semen samples.

▶ **Evaluation:** The model was evaluated using precision, recall, and F1 score, which are commonly used metrics for object counting tasks. The model achieved high scores on all metrics, indicating that it is effective at accurately counting sperm in the semen videos.

▶ **Use Cases:** This model can be used in clinical or research settings to quickly and accurately count sperm in semen samples. This can be useful for diagnosing and monitoring male infertility, as well as for understanding the impact of various factors on sperm count.

▶ **Limits and Risks:** The model is only trained to count sperm in semen videos taken under a microscope and may not perform well on videos taken under different conditions or with different types of microscopes. It is important to ensure that the semen samples are of high quality and that the video recording conditions are consistent in order to obtain accurate results.

▶ **Common Myths or Misunderstandings:** This model is not intended to replace human expert judgment and should be used as a tool to support decision making. The results generated by this model are not a substitute for professional medical advice, diagnosis, or treatment. Overall I'd say this model is not too scary, models like these might be best deployed as front-line diagnosis and ranking tools for patients who otherwise would not be receiving care. The main issue that might appear is any editorializing that might occur by the machine learning engineers training this model. Imagine that this model was only trained on young white men (graduate student volunteers) and the shape and size of sperm changes across ages or races. This type of bias in training data appears frequently in medical models, especially skin cancer models[25].

▶ **Quality Grade:** B+

▶ **Cost to Create:** $100,000

▶ **Creator's Note:** If you can collect good labeled videos of sperm with their counts, you can make this model. It would be hard for anyone to steal it unless they had access to your raw data, and also be very hard for anyone to know that you are using a model to count sperm instead of a human eyeball under a microscope. I think this model and many medical models like this are neat, and also worry that if we don't let doctors use them explicitly they will do it behind our backs.

5.2.11 *Handwriting Recognizer*

▶ **Description:** The Handwriting Classifier is a type of machine learning model that's designed to recognize and classify handwriting. It can be trained on a dataset of handwritten text and images, and can then be used to identify the writer of a given sample of handwriting or to classify handwriting by writer, writing style, or content. The model can be based on a variety of machine learning algorithms, including deep learning, support vector machines, or decision trees.

▶ **Training Data:** The Handwriting Classifier is typically trained on a large dataset of handwritten text and images, which can include a diverse range of writing styles, writers, and content. The quality and quantity of the training data will impact the performance of the model, so it's important to use a diverse and representative dataset that accurately represents the range of handwriting styles and content.

▶ **Evaluation:** The performance of the Handwriting Classifier can be evaluated using a variety of metrics, such as accuracy, precision, recall, and F1 score. These metrics can be used to compare different models and to track the progress of a model as it's trained on more data. Additionally, the model can be validated using independent test data that was not used during training, to assess its ability to generalize to new, unseen handwriting.

▶ **Use Cases:** The Handwriting Classifier has a number of potential use cases, including:
  1. Identifying the writer of a given sample of handwriting
  2. Classifying handwriting by writer, writing style, or content
  3. Supporting forensic and legal investigations by providing evidence in handwriting analysis
  4. Enhancing handwriting recognition in products and services, such as digital note-taking and document management systems

▶ **Limits and Risks:** Like any machine learning model, the Handwriting Classifier has limitations and risks. One of the main limitations is that it may not always be accurate, and may misclassify handwriting or misidentify the writer. Additionally, the model may be biased toward certain writing styles, writers, or content if the training data is not representative of the range of handwriting styles and content.

▶ **Common Myths or Misunderstandings:** There are a few common myths or misunderstandings about the Handwriting Classifier. One myth is that the model can always accurately identify the writer of a given sample of handwriting, when in reality it can only provide a prediction based on the information it was trained on. Another myth is that the model can replace human expertise and judgment in handwriting analysis (don't use this model in court to prove that two pieces of handwriting are the same, it can't explain itself and you'll end up getting appealed by the innocence project[26].

▶ **Quality Grade:** A-

▶ **Cost to Create:** $10,000-$100,000

▶ **Creator's Note:** If this model only needs to classify handwriting and convert it to text, it's not too hard to make and copy. If, however, it needs to accurately identify the writer of a given sample of handwriting, it's much harder to make and copy.

5.2.12 *Drug Discovery*

▶ **Description:** The Liver Drug Discovery Model is a type of machine learning model that's designed to predict the potential efficacy and toxicity of drugs for the liver. It can be trained on a dataset of drug and liver data, including information about drug structure, pharmacokinetics, and pharmacodynamics, as well as liver function, anatomy, and physiology. The model can then be used to predict the potential impact of a given drug on the liver and to identify drugs that may be suitable for liver-related diseases.

▶ **Training Data:** The Liver Drug Discovery Model is typically trained on a large dataset of drug and liver data, which can include both experimental and observational data. The size and quality of the training data will impact the performance of the model, so it's important to use a diverse and representative dataset that accurately represents the relationships between drugs and the liver.

▶ **Evaluation:** The performance of the Liver Drug Discovery Model can be evaluated using a variety of metrics, such as accuracy, precision, recall, and F1 score. These metrics can be used to compare different models and to track the progress of a model as it's trained on more data. Additionally, the model can be validated using independent test data that was not used during training, to assess its ability to generalize to new, unseen data.

▶ **Use Cases:** The Liver Drug Discovery Model has a number of potential use cases, including:
1. Predicting the potential efficacy and toxicity of drugs for the liver
2. Supporting drug discovery and development by identifying promising drug candidates for liver- related diseases
3. Enhancing drug safety by identifying potential liver-related side effects of drugs
4. Supporting liver research and education by providing insights into liver function and drug interactions

▶ **Limits and Risks:** Like any machine learning model, the Liver Drug Discovery Model has limitations and risks. One of the main limitations is that it may not always make accurate predictions, and may miss important relationships between drugs and the liver. Additionally, the model may be biased toward certain drugs, liver functions, or disease conditions if the training data is not representative of the relationships between drugs and the liver.

▶ **Common Myths or Misunderstandings:** There are a few common myths or misunderstandings about the Liver Drug Discovery Model. One myth is that the model can always accurately predict the potential efficacy and toxicity of drugs for the liver, when in reality it can only provide a prediction based on the information it was trained on[27]. Another myth is that the model can replace human expertise and judgment in drug discovery and development, when in reality it is intended to support and enhance human decision-making processes. Like the fluid dynamics model, this model will be very useful when deployed as part of the creative process of decision making regarding drugs, but shouldn't make any critical decisions by itself.

▶ **Quality Grade:** B+

▶ **Cost to Create:** $500,000

▶ **Creator's Note:** This model is very similar to the fluid dynamics model, but it is adding an additional step in guessing the interaction of the final drug with the liver. This is a very difficult problem but if you had a good dataset of past drug trials, it could have a go. The model will probably not be highly accurate, but considering how many drugs fail it doesn't need to be. If the model gives reasonable suggestions for drug candidates it will be a boom for the company deploying it. As far as detectability goes, I think a drug company could use this model to find drugs and keep it a secret and no one would know.

5.2.13 *Autism*

▶ **Description:** The Autism Classifier is a type of machine learning model that's designed to predict the likelihood of autism in children. It can be trained on a dataset of behavioral and physiological data, such as eye gaze patterns, facial expressions, and vocalizations, as well as demographic information. The model can then be used to identify children who may be at risk for autism and to support early diagnosis and intervention.

▶ **Training Data:** The Autism Classifier is typically trained on a large dataset of behavioral and physiological data, as well as demographic information. The size and quality of the training data will impact the performance of the model, so it's important to use a diverse and representative dataset that accurately represents the characteristics of children with and without autism.

▶ **Evaluation:** The performance of the Autism Classifier can be evaluated using a variety of metrics, such as accuracy, precision, recall, and F1 score. These metrics can be used to compare different models and to track the progress of a model as it's trained on more data. Additionally, the model can be validated using independent test data that was not used during training, to assess its ability to generalize to new, unseen data.

▶ **Use Cases:** The Autism Classifier has a number of potential use cases, including:
  1. Identifying children who may be at risk for autism
  2. Supporting early diagnosis and intervention for autism
  3. Enhancing autism research and education by providing insights into autism symptoms and characteristics

▶ **Limits and Risks:** Like any machine learning model, the Autism Classifier has limitations and risks. One of the main limitations is that it may not always be accurate, and may misclassify children or misidentify the likelihood of autism. Additionally, the model may be biased toward certain demographic groups, behavioral and physiological characteristics, or autism symptoms if the training data is not representative of the characteristics of children with and without autism.

▶ **Common Myths or Misunderstandings:** [28] There are a few common myths or misunderstandings about the Autism Classifier. One myth is that the model can always accurately identify children who may be at risk for autism, when in reality it can only provide a prediction based on the information it was trained on. This one is tough and there are a few issues at play. First, this model may appear to work, but remember it cannot explain why it made the classification it did, also it suffers from the same issue of editorializing that the sperm counter or skin cancer model might face. With these things in mind it might be an incredibly useful tool if deployed as a cheap self-check for worried parents. However, one would need to be careful how the model accuracy is reported in order to establish user's trust, reporting false-positive and false-negative rates would be very important, and even if they were reported each false-positive (or false-negative) might cause a panic and lead to huge reputational damage to the modelers.

▶ **Quality Grade:** C

▶ **Cost to Create:** $100,000

▶ **Creator's Note:** This model depends on a large and varying dataset, and helps diagnose a disorder that is famously on a spectrum. Given all of that this model would be fairly hard to exactly copy, but would also be fairly inaccurate and probably easy to fool. This model is an interesting idea but probably not as straightforward to use as a skin cancer detection model, where the disease is surface-level and well understood.

5.2.14 *Online Dating*

▶ **Description:** The Online Dating Matcher is a type of machine learning model that's designed to match individuals for online dating. It can be trained on a dataset of user profiles, including demographic information, preferences, and interests. The model can then be used to recommend potential matches based on compatibility and to support the process of finding a romantic partner online.

▶ **Training Data:** The Online Dating Matcher is typically trained on a large dataset of user profiles, which can include both explicit and implicit information about individuals and their preferences. The size and quality of the training data will impact the performance of the model, so it's important to use a diverse and representative dataset that accurately represents the range of individuals and preferences in the online dating population.

▶ **Evaluation:** The performance of the Online Dating Matcher can be evaluated using a variety of metrics, such as accuracy, precision, recall, and F1 score. These metrics can be used to compare different models and to track the progress of a model as it's trained on more data. Additionally, the model can be validated using independent test data that was not used during training, to assess its ability to generalize to new, unseen user profiles.

▶ **Use Cases:** The Online Dating Matcher has a number of potential use cases, including:
  1. 1.Recommending potential matches based on compatibility
  2. 2.Supporting the process of finding a romantic partner online
  3. 3. Enhancing online dating research and education by providing insights into online dating preferences and behaviors

▶ **Limits and Risks:** Like any machine learning model, the Online Dating Matcher has limitations and risks. One of the main limitations is that it may not always make accurate recommendations, and may miss important relationships between individuals and their preferences. Additionally, the model may be biased toward certain demographic groups, preferences, or interests if the training data is not representative of the range of individuals and preferences in the online dating population.

▶ **Common Myths or Misunderstandings:** There are a few common myths or misunderstandings about the Online Dating Matcher. One myth is that the model can always accurately recommend potential matches based on compatibility, when in reality it can only provide a prediction based on the information it was trained on. There is also a big opportunity for editorializing with this model. Some nerd might hijack this model and train it on a nonrepresentative sample in an attempt to get their friends successfully matched. It also would have a hard time explaining why it matched a couple.

▶ **Quality Grade:** B+

▶ **Cost to Create:** $50,000

▶ **Creator's Note:** This model can be generalized from a relatively small dataset, it also could be ensembled to match people based on common interests. Once people are willing to try this model it will rapidly improve. If the model results are public, this model will be easy to steal, but would be hard to detect if someone is using it given the variance in matches in dating.

5.2.15 *Online Advertising*

▶ **Description:** The Online Ad Server Classifier is a type of machine learning model that's designed to classify online ads as appropriate for the current user or unsafe. It can be trained on a dataset of ad content, including text, images, and videos, as well as information about the ad server. The model can then be used to identify unsafe ads and to support the process of filtering out inappropriate content.

▶ **Training Data:** The Online Ad Server Classifier is typically trained on a large dataset of ad content, which can include both explicit and implicit information about ads and their content. The size and quality of the training data will impact the performance of the model, so it's important to use a diverse and representative dataset that accurately represents the range of ads and ad content.

▶ **Evaluation:** The performance of the Online Ad Server Classifier can be evaluated using a variety of metrics, such as accuracy, precision, recall, and F1 score. These metrics can be used to compare different models and to track the progress of a model as it's trained on more data. Additionally, the model can be validated using independent test data that was not used during training, to assess its ability to generalize to new, unseen ad content.

▶ **Use Cases:** The Online Ad Server Classifier has a number of potential use cases, including:
1. Identifying unsafe ads
2. Supporting the process of filtering out inappropriate content
3. Enhancing online ad research and education by providing insights into online ad content and characteristics

▶ **Limits and Risks:** Like any machine learning model, the Online Ad Server Classifier has limitations and risks. One of the main limitations is that it may not always be accurate, and may misclassify ads or misidentify the likelihood of safety. Additionally, the model may be biased towards certain demographic groups, ad content, or ad characteristics if the training data is not representative of the range of ads and ad content.

▶ **Common Myths or Misunderstandings:** Online advertising models are all marketed the same way, but the underlying data that comes from a small dataset (from a few publishers) or a large one (one from an ad exchange) means their efficacy can vary wildly. Concept drift is the most common problem as not all products or services in advertising are created equal. An advertisement meant to build brand awareness for Accenture should be ran very differently than an advertisement to buy caffeinated shampoo from Amazon. The AI will optimize for the parameters that it is told to optimize for and the concept of success for an advertisement changes by the product and sometimes over time as distribution channels or business models change.

▶ **Quality Grade:** B+

▶ **Cost to Create:** $100,000

▶ **Creator's Note:** Models like these are ubiquitous and are used by all major ad exchanges and publishers. The data is proprietary, but fairly easy to collect from the open web (you can scrape webpages and see what types of ads show up on them) so the models are easily copied. The models are not hard to detect if they are being used, especially if they are highly targeted.

5.2.16 *Tennis*

▶ **Description:** The Tennis Playing Bot is a type of machine learning model that's designed to play the game of tennis. It can be trained on a dataset of tennis data, including information about court geometry, ball trajectory, and player behavior. The model can then be used to play tennis against other players or bots, either in simulation or in real-world settings.

▶ **Training Data:** The Tennis Playing Bot is typically trained on a large dataset of tennis data, which can include both expert demonstrations and self-play data. The size and quality of the training data will impact the performance of the model, so it's important to use a diverse and representative dataset that accurately represents the range of tennis strategies and tactics.

▶ **Evaluation:** The performance of the Tennis Playing Bot can be evaluated using a variety of metrics, such as win rate, average length of rallies, and percentage of successful shots. These metrics can be used to compare different models and to track the progress of a model as it's trained on more data. Additionally, the model can be validated using independent test data that was not used during training, to assess its ability to generalize to new, unseen tennis situations.

▶ **Use Cases:** The Tennis Playing Bot has a number of potential use cases, including:
1. Playing tennis against other players or bots, either in simulation or in real-world settings
2. Supporting tennis research and education by providing insights into the strategies and tactics used in the game
3. Enhancing the user experience of tennis gaming

▶ **Limits and Risks:** Like any machine learning model, the Tennis Playing Bot has limitations and risks. One of the main limitations is that it may not always be accurate, and may make mistakes or misinterpret the game of tennis. Additionally, the model may be biased toward certain demographic groups, tennis strategies, or tennis tactics if the training data is not representative of the range of tennis strategies and tactics.

▶ **Common Myths or Misunderstandings:** There are a few common myths or misunderstandings about the Tennis Playing Bot. One myth is that the model can always accurately play tennis against other players or bots, when in reality it can only provide a prediction based on the information it was trained on. Another common misunderstanding is where the computational difficulty lies, predicting where a ball will go is actually computationally easy, but holding the racquet and coordinating movement and balance might be the hard part

▶ **Quality Grade:** C

▶ **Cost to Create:** $400,000

▶ **Creator's Note:** This one might surprise people, but the Tennis Playing Bot is actually very difficult to copy. This is mostly a technical constraint that getting a bot to stand, move and hold a tennis racquet will be the hardest part. If this were a "Video Game Tennis Playing Bot" this would be almost free to make. It's a pedantic point but a fun one that is important to think about when deciding to work on a ML problem.

5.2.17 *Hate Speech*

▶ **Description:** The Hate Speech Classifier is a type of machine learning model that's designed to identify hate speech in text. It can be trained on a dataset of text data, including examples of hate speech and non-hate speech. The model can then be used to automatically identify and flag hate speech in online forums, social media, and other text-based platforms.

▶ **Training Data:** The Hate Speech Classifier is typically trained on a large dataset of text data, which can include both explicit and implicit examples of hate speech and non-hate speech. The size and quality of the training data will impact the performance of the model, so it's important to use a diverse and representative dataset that accurately represents the range of hate speech and non-hate speech in the target platform.

▶ **Evaluation:** The performance of the Hate Speech Classifier can be evaluated using a variety of metrics, such as accuracy, precision, recall, and F1 score. These metrics can be used to compare different models and to track the progress of a model as it's trained on more data. Additionally, the model can be validated using independent test data that was not used during training, to assess its ability to generalize to new, unseen text data.

▶ **Use Cases:** The Hate Speech Classifier has a number of potential use cases, including:
1. Identifying hate speech in online forums, social media, and other text-based platforms
2. Supporting the process of filtering out inappropriate content
3. Enhancing online research and education by providing insights into online text data and characteristics

▶ **Limits and Risks:** Like any machine learning model, the Hate Speech Classifier has limitations and risks. One of the main limitations is that it may not always be accurate, and may misclassify text data or misidentify the likelihood of hate speech. Additionally, the model may be biased toward certain demographic groups, text data, or text characteristics if the training data is not representative of the range of hate speech and non-hate speech.

▶ **Common Myths or Misunderstandings:** There are a few common myths or misunderstandings about the Hate Speech Classifier. One myth is that the model can always accurately identify hate speech in online forums, social media, and other text. As we've seen in many models with a social component, concept driftlooms large, language evolves over time, and sometimes language evolves explicitly to get around auto-moderators, so the model can affect the user input thus increasing the speed of change. There is also on opportunity to editorialize that is very hard to overcome, and any attempt to edit the training set might be labeled as "woke AI"[29] or called similar names by whatever interest group is affected by the training dataset.

▶ **Quality Grade:** C

▶ **Cost to Create:** $1,000,000

▶ **Creator's Note:** What is hate speech anyway? This model can be made but it's hard to define what hate speech is, and it's hard to define what is not hate speech. If you think it is easy consider that Facebook pays $500 million per year to Accenture to moderate hate speech on its site.[30]

5.2.18 *Fake News*

▶ **Description:** The Fake News Classifier is a type of machine learning model that's designed to identify fake news in text. It can be trained on a dataset of text data, including examples of fake news and real news. The model can then be used to automatically identify and flag fake news in online news sources, social media, and other text-based platforms.

▶ **Training Data:** The Fake News Classifier is typically trained on a large dataset of text data, which can include both explicit and implicit examples of fake news and real news. The size and quality of the training data will impact the performance of the model, so it's important to use a diverse and representative dataset that accurately represents the range of fake news and real news in the target platform.

▶ **Evaluation:** The performance of the Fake News Classifier can be evaluated using a variety of metrics, such as accuracy, precision, recall, and F1 score. These metrics can be used to compare different models and to track the progress of a model as it's trained on more data. Additionally, the model can be validated using independent test data that was not used during training, to assess its ability to generalize to new, unseen text data.

▶ **Use Cases:** The Fake News Classifier has a number of potential use cases, including:
1. Identifying fake news in online news sources, social media, and other text-based platforms
2. Supporting the process of filtering out inappropriate content
3. Enhancing online research and education by providing insights into online text data and characteristics

▶ **Limits and Risks:** Like any machine learning model, the Fake News Classifier has limitations and risks. One of the main limitations is that it may not always be accurate, and may misclassify text data or misidentify the likelihood of fake news. Additionally, the model may be biased toward certain demographic groups, text data, or text characteristics if the training data is not representative of the range of fake news and real news.

▶ **Common Myths or Misunderstandings:** There are a few common myths or misunderstandings about the Fake News Classifier. One myth is that the model can always accurately identify fake news in online news sources, social media, and other text-based platforms, when in reality it can only provide a prediction based on the information it was trained on and may miss important examples of fake news. Another myth is that the model can replace human expertise and judgment in evaluating news sources, when in reality it is intended to support and enhance human decision-making processes. The problems of concept drift and editorializing show themselves here just as in the hate speech model above. An outlet that needs to explain why certain content is not allowed will have trouble codifying its rules if a deep learning model is used because of the inherent lack of explainability which means that the model might act as a tool used in the (somewhat creative) process but the critical decisions must still be made by humans who can give explicit reasons.

▶ **Quality Grade:** C

▶ **Cost to Create:** $1,000,000

▶ **Creator's Note:** Just like hate speech, it is very hard to pin down a stable definition of fake news. This model would be useful but it is practically very difficult to make.

5.2.19 *Legal Contracts*

▶ **Description:** The Contract Review Bot is a type of machine learning model that's designed to support the process of contract review. It can be trained on a dataset of contract data, including examples of well-written and poorly-written contracts, as well as relevant legal and business terms. The model can then be used to automatically review contracts and identify potential issues, such as missing information, ambiguous language, and non-compliant terms.

▶ **Training Data:** The Contract Review Bot is typically trained on a large dataset of contract data, which can include both expert-annotated and self-generated data. The size and quality of the training data will impact the performance of the model, so it's important to use a diverse and representative dataset that accurately represents the range of contracts and legal and business terms in the target domain.

▶ **Evaluation:** The performance of the Contract Review Bot can be evaluated using a variety of metrics, such as accuracy, precision, recall, and F1 score. These metrics can be used to compare different models and to track the progress of a model as it's trained on more data. Additionally, the model can be validated using independent test data that was not used during training, to assess its ability to generalize to new, unseen contracts.

▶ **Use Cases:** The Contract Review Bot has a number of potential use cases, including:
1. Supporting the process of contract review
2. Enhancing online research and education by providing insights into online contract data and characteristics

▶ **Limits and Risks:** Like any machine learning model, the Contract Review Bot has limitations and risks. One of the main limitations is that it may not always be accurate, and may misclassify contract data or misidentify the likelihood of potential issues. Additionally, the model may be biased toward certain demographic groups, contract data, or contract characteristics if the training data is not representative of the range of contracts and legal and business terms.

▶ **Common Myths or Misunderstandings:** There are a few common myths or misunderstandings about the Contract Review Bot. One myth is that the model can always accurately review contracts and identify potential issues, when in reality it can only provide a prediction based on the information it was trained on and may miss important issues. Another myth is that the model can replace human expertise and judgment in contract review, when in reality it is intended to support and enhance human decision-making processes. Again we find concept drift being a potential issue here, although maybe less so if logical legal language changes more slowly than other written text. The model may still not pick up on the latest legal hacks that are snuck into contracts unless explicitly trained on data to recognize them.

▶ **Quality Grade:** A-

▶ **Cost to Create:** $100,000+

▶ **Creator's Note:** I love this model. Many legal contracts are in the public domain, as are judgments relating to them. Making this model, and copying it is very cheap considering how powerful the resulting model would be. Legal text is made carefully (in general) and is often very verbose and thorough, which is a perfect scenario for a machine learning problem.

5.2.20 *Facial Recognition*

▶ **Description:** Facial Recognition is a type of machine learning model that's designed to identify individuals based on their facial features. It can be trained on a dataset of facial images, including images of people and their corresponding identities. The model can then be used to recognize individuals in new images, such as those captured by cameras or uploaded to social media.

▶ **Training Data:** Facial Recognition models are typically trained on large datasets of facial images, which can include images from a variety of sources, such as social media, public datasets, and private collections. The size and diversity of the training data will impact the performance of the model, so it's important to use a representative and diverse dataset that accurately captures the range of facial features and demographics of the target population.

▶ **Evaluation:** The performance of Facial Recognition models can be evaluated using a variety of metrics, such as accuracy, precision, recall, and F1 score. These metrics can be used to compare different models and to track the progress of a model as it's trained on more data. Additionally, the model can be validated using independent test data that was not used during training, to assess its ability to generalize to new, unseen faces.

▶ **Use Cases:** Facial Recognition models have a number of potential use cases, including:
1. Identifying individuals in new images, such as those captured by cameras or uploaded to social media
2. Supporting the process of filtering out inappropriate content
3. Enhancing online research and education by providing insights into online facial images and characteristics

▶ **Limits and Risks:** Like any machine learning model, Facial Recognition models have limitations and risks. One of the main limitations is that they may not always be accurate, and may misclassify facial images or misidentify the identity of individuals. Additionally, the model may be biased toward certain demographic groups, facial images, or facial characteristics if the training data is not representative of the range of facial features and demographics.

▶ **Common Myths or Misunderstandings:** There are a couple of common myths or misunderstandings about Facial Recognition models. One myth is that the models can always accurately identify individuals, when in reality they can only provide a prediction based on the information they were trained on and may miss important facial features or misidentify individuals. Another myth is that the models can replace human judgment and expertise in identifying individuals, when in reality they are intended to support and enhance human decision-making processes. If we want a model that recognizes everyone in the world, we need to retrain that model every time a new baby is born, or and when people get plastic surgery, and when they wear elaborate makeup;concept drift is everywhere in this model.

▶ **Quality Grade:** B

▶ **Cost to Create:** $10,000-$1,000,000

▶ **Creator's Note:** There are many versions of this model out in the world; to get a reasonable one might cost $10,000 and use public data. To get a CIA or Chinese government level one might cost $1 million or more and use private data.

5.2.21 *Smartwatches*

▶ **Description:** The Smartwatch Danger Classifier is a type of machine learning model that's designed to identify potential dangers faced by smartwatch wearers. It can be trained on a dataset of smartwatch data, including information about physiological signals, activity patterns, and environmental conditions. The model can then be used to automatically detect and alert smartwatch wearers of potential dangers, such as falls, heart attacks, and other health emergencies.

▶ **Training Data:** The Smartwatch Danger Classifier is typically trained on a large dataset of smartwatch data, which can include data from a variety of sources, such as clinical studies, self-reported data, and wearable sensors. The size and quality of the training data will impact the performance of the model, so it's important to use a diverse and representative dataset that accurately represents the range of physiological signals, activity patterns, and environmental conditions faced by smartwatch wearers.

▶ **Evaluation:** The performance of the Smartwatch Danger Classifier can be evaluated using a variety of metrics, such as accuracy, precision, recall, and F1 score. These metrics can be used to compare different models and to track the progress of a model as it's trained on more data. Additionally, the model can be validated using independent test data that was not used during training, to assess its ability to generalize to new, unseen smartwatch data.

▶ **Use Cases:** The Smartwatch Danger Classifier has a number of potential use cases, including:
1. Automatically detecting and alerting smartwatch wearers of potential dangers, such as falls, heart attacks, and other health emergencies
2. Supporting the process of filtering out inappropriate content

3. Enhancing online research and education by providing insights into online smartwatch data and characteristics

▶ **Limits and Risks:** Like any machine learning model, the Smartwatch Danger Classifier has limitations and risks. One of the main limitations is that it may not always be accurate, and may misclassify smartwatch data or misidentify the likelihood of potential dangers. Additionally, the model may be biased toward certain demographic groups, smartwatch data, or smartwatch characteristics if the training data is not representative of the range of physiological signals, activity patterns, and environmental conditions.

▶ **Common Myths or Misunderstandings:** There are a few common myths or misunderstandings about the Smartwatch Wearer Danger Classifier. One myth is that the model can always accurately identify dangers, when in reality it can only provide a prediction based on the information it was trained on and may miss important signals or trigger false alarms[31]. Another myth is that the model can replace human judgment and expertise in evaluating personal safety, when in reality it is intended to support and enhance human decision-making processes. On the smartwatch of a healthy person, the AI making the critical decision to call 911 is probably a mistake, as a "Life Alert" type device on an elderly person or anyone deemed sufficiently at risk, this model may be deployed effectively to help alert their caregivers. With this in mind there is an opportunity for accidental editorializing if a model made for elderly emergency alerts is trained on young people, or vice-versa.

▶ **Quality Grade:** B

▶ **Cost to Create:** $100,000

▶ **Creator's Note:** A model like this is easy to make, but hard to get right. The false positives and false negatives are very important, and the model needs to be trained on a diverse dataset to avoid bias.

5.2.22 *Threat Detection*

▶ **Description:** The CCTV Threat Classifier is a type of machine learning model that's designed to identify potential threats in video footage captured by closed-circuit television (CCTV) cameras. It can be trained on a dataset of video data, including examples of normal and abnormal activity, such as criminal behavior, accidents, and other incidents. The model can then be used to automatically monitor video footage and alert security personnel of potential threats.

▶ **Training Data:** The CCTV Threat Classifier is typically trained on a large dataset of video data, which can include data from a variety of sources, such as public safety agencies, security cameras, and other sources. The size and quality of the training data will impact the performance of the model, so it's important to use a diverse and representative dataset that accurately represents the range of normal and abnormal activity in the target environment.

▶ **Evaluation:** The performance of the CCTV Threat Classifier can be evaluated using a variety of metrics, such as accuracy, precision, recall, and F1 score. These metrics can be used to compare different models and to track the progress of a model as it's trained on more data.

▶ **Use Cases:** The CCTV Threat Classifier has a number of potential use cases, including:
1. Automatically detecting and alerting security personnel of potential threats, such as criminal behavior, accidents, and other incidents
2. Supporting the process of filtering out inappropriate content
3. Enhancing online research and education by providing insights into online video data and characteristics

110

▶ **Limits and Risks:** Like any machine learning model, the CCTV Threat Classifier has limitations and risks. One of the main limitations is that it may not always be accurate, and may misclassify video data or misidentify the likelihood of potential threats. Additionally, the model may be biased toward certain demographic groups, video data, or video characteristics if the training data is not representative of the range of normal and abnormal activity.

▶ **Common Myths or Misunderstandings:** There are a few common myths or misunderstandings about the CCTV Threat Classifier. One myth is that the model can always accurately identify threats, when in reality it can only provide a prediction based on the information it was trained on and may miss important signals or trigger false alarms. Another myth is that the model can replace human judgment and expertise in evaluating security threats, when in reality it is intended to support and enhance human decision-making processes[32]. This model suffers from all of the usual suspects; what it means to be a threat might drift over time and geography, datasets may be editorialized to cause more false positives or negatives depending on the bias in the dataset and of course any decisions made by this model will be largely unexplainable. These risks aside, a model can be deployed as part of the decision making process, but letting it make critical decisions by itself would be a mistake. Models like this are the core of autonomous weapons and self-driving cars, which I will discuss in chapters 6 and 7.

▶ **Quality Grade:** B

▶ **Cost to Create:** $100,000+

▶ **Creator's Note:** Concept drift is one to really look out for here; does the threat change to avoid detection? If so, then you are in trouble if you rely on this model.

5.2.23 *University Admissions*

▶ **Description:** The Harvard University Student Acceptance Bot is a type of machine learning model that's designed to automate the process of evaluating applications from prospective students for admission to a university. It can be trained on a dataset of student applications, including information about academic records, test scores, essays, and other factors. The model can then be used to automatically evaluate new applications and accept or reject students based on their qualifications.

▶ **Training Data:** The Harvard University Student Acceptance Bot is typically trained on a large dataset of student applications, which can include data from a variety of sources, such as universities, testing organizations, and other sources. The size and quality of the training data will impact the performance of the model, so it's important to use a diverse and representative dataset that accurately represents the range of academic records, test scores, essays, and other factors used to evaluate student applications.

▶ **Evaluation:** The performance of the Harvard University Student Acceptance Bot can be evaluated using a variety of metrics, such as accuracy, precision, recall, and F1 score. These metrics can be used to compare different models and to track the progress of a model as it's trained on more data. Additionally, the model can be validated using independent test data that was not used during training, to assess its ability to generalize to new, unseen student applications.

▶ **Use Cases:** The Harvard University Student Acceptance Bot has a number of potential use cases, including:
1. Automating the process of evaluating student applications for admission to a university
2. Streamlining the admission process and reducing the time and effort required to manually evaluate applications
3. Supporting fair and objective decision-making by reducing the impact of human biases and subjectivity

4. Supporting research and education by providing insights into the academic records, test scores, essays, and other factors that are most predictive of student success

▶ **Limits and Risks:** Like any machine learning model, the Harvard University Student Acceptance Bot has limitations and risks. One of the main limitations is that it may not always make accurate predictions, and may overlook important qualifications or reject qualified students. Additionally, the model may be biased toward certain academic records, test scores, essays, or demographic groups if the training data is not representative of the range of factors used to evaluate student applications.

▶ **Common Myths or Misunderstandings:** There are a few common myths or misunderstandings about the Harvard University Student Acceptance Bot. One myth is that the model can always accurately evaluate student applications, when in reality it can only provide a prediction based on the information it was trained on and may overlook important qualifications or reject qualified students. Another myth is that the model can replace human judgment and expertise in evaluating student applications, when in reality it is intended to support and enhance human decision-making processes. This model looks exactly like the online dating model, in that its outputs will be unexplainable and subject to editorializing; additionally there may be a large amount of concept drift if what it means to be a "good" student changes over time.

▶ **Quality Grade:** C

▶ **Cost to Create:** $50,000

▶ **Creator's Note:** This model is similar to the online dating model, but worse. Many university admissions processes are opaque and I'm sure if some universities had to programmatically codify their biases they would get into big legal trouble (more than they already have).

5.2.24 *Credit Score*

▶ **Description:** The Simple Credit Score is a type of machine learning model that's designed to predict an individual's creditworthiness based on financial and demographic information. It can be trained on a dataset of credit information, including information about payment history, income, employment, and other factors. The model can then be used to automatically calculate a credit score for an individual and make predictions about their likelihood of defaulting on a loan.

▶ **Training Data:** The Simple Credit Score is typically trained on a large dataset of credit information, which can include data from a variety of sources, such as credit bureaus, financial institutions, and other sources. The size and quality of the training data will impact the performance of the model, so it's important to use a diverse and representative dataset that accurately represents the range of credit information for the target population.

▶ **Evaluation:** The performance of the Simple Credit Score can be evaluated using a variety of metrics, such as accuracy, precision, recall, and F1 score. These metrics can be used to compare different models and to track the progress of a model as it's trained on more data. Additionally, the model can be validated using independent test data that was not used during training, to assess its ability to generalize to new, unseen credit information.

▶ **Use Cases:** The Simple Credit Score has a number of potential use cases, including:
1. Automatically calculating a credit score for an individual based on financial and demographic information
2. Supporting fair and objective decision-making in the lending process by reducing the impact of human biases and subjectivity
3. Enhancing the efficiency of the lending process by reducing the time and effort required to manually evaluate credit information
4. Supporting research and education by providing insights into the financial and demographic factors that are most predictive of creditworthiness

▶ **Limits and Risks:** Like any machine learning model, the Simple Credit Score has limitations and risks. One of the main limitations is that it may not always make accurate predictions, and may overlook important factors or make incorrect predictions about creditworthiness. Additionally, the model may be biased toward certain financial and demographic factors if the training data is not representative of the range of credit information for the target population.

▶ **Common Myths or Misunderstandings:** There are a few common myths or misunderstandings about the Simple Credit Score. One myth is that the model can always accurately predict creditworthiness, when in reality it can only provide a prediction based on the information it was trained on and may overlook important factors or make incorrect predictions. Another myth is that the model can replace human judgment and expertise in evaluating creditworthiness, when in reality it is intended to support and enhance human decision-making processes. A simple credit score might not experience weekly concept drift, what it means to pay your bills on time does not change often, but if the input data is behavioral then concept drift might be acute and frequent if the job of this model is to flag the people with money as being creditworthy based on their behavior, your static model will break every time their behavior changes. It also might be a risk that your customers game the model in a similar way that a hate speech model can be gamed, if it is found out that if you shop at a farmers market then the model predicts you are credit-worthy, then your customers with poor credit might start shopping at farmers markets to improve your score, and thus break your model.

▶ **Quality Grade:** B+

▶ **Cost to Create:** $100,000

▶ **Creator's Note:** Keep models like this simple, but make many versions of them and ensemble them together with humans to make your decision.

5.2.25 *Social Credit Score*

▶ **Description:** The Social Credit Score is a type of machine learning model that's designed to predict an individual's trustworthiness based on their social behavior and online activities. It can be trained on a dataset of social and online information, including information about online interactions, reputation, and other factors. The model can then be used to automatically calculate a social credit score for an individual and make predictions about their trustworthiness.

▶ **Training Data:** The Social Credit Score is typically trained on a large dataset of social and online information, which can include data from a variety of sources, such as social media, online communities, and other sources. The size and quality of the training data will impact the performance of the model, so it's important to use a diverse and representative dataset that accurately represents the range of social and online information for the target population.

▶ **Evaluation:** The performance of the Social Credit Score can be evaluated using a variety of metrics, such as accuracy, precision, recall, and F1 score. These metrics can be used to compare different models and to track the progress of a model as it's trained on more data. Additionally, the model can be validated using independent test data that was not used during training, to assess its ability to generalize to new, unseen social and online information.

▶ **Use Cases:** The Social Credit Score has a number of potential use cases, including:
1. Automatically calculating a social credit score for an individual based on their social behavior and online activities
2. Supporting fair and objective decision-making in the lending process by reducing the impact of human biases and subjectivity
3. Enhancing the efficiency of the lending process by reducing the time and effort required to manually evaluate social and online information
4. Supporting research and education by providing insights

into the social behavior and online activities that are most predictive of trustworthiness

▶ **Limits and Risks:** Like any machine learning model, the Social Credit Score has limitations and risks. One of the main limitations is that it may not always make accurate predictions, and may overlook important factors or make incorrect predictions about trustworthiness. Additionally, the model may be biased toward certain social behavior and online activities if the training data is not representative of the range of social and online information for the target population.

▶ **Common Myths or Misunderstandings:** There are a few common myths or misunderstandings about the Social Credit Score. One myth is that the model can always accurately predict trustworthiness, when in reality it can only provide a prediction based on the information it was trained on and may overlook important factors or make incorrect predictions. Another myth is that the model can replace human judgment and expertise in evaluating trustworthiness, when in reality it is intended to support and enhance human decision-making processes. This model is included almost as a joke, but this is something that is seriously being attempted by governments and private companies, the model suffers from almost every sucker trap; it's likely to encode the creators bias, acting as a large editorial on society, the outputs would be unexplainable in court, social concepts change rapidly so concept drift would be ever-present and it would be foolish to rely on it for any critical decision making. Using a model like this would be akin to deploying a toy online dating model but then determining many aspects of people's lives based on that one model. It might be interesting to discuss, but it would be foolish.

▶ ▶**Quality Grade:** F

▶ ▶ **Cost to Create:** $1,000,000,000

▶ ▶**Creator's Note:** Don't make this model.

5.2.26 *AGI*

▶ **Description:** The Artificial General Intelligence (AGI) Chatbot is a type of machine learning model that's designed to simulate human-like conversation with users. It can be trained on a large dataset of text, including examples of human conversation, to learn how to generate appropriate and coherent responses to a wide range of topics and questions. The model can then be used to engage in natural language conversation with users, providing answers and insights on a variety of topics.

▶ **Training Data:** The AGI Chatbot is typically trained on a large dataset of text, which can include data from a variety of sources, such as books, websites, and other sources. The size and quality of the training data will impact the performance of the model, so it's important to use a diverse and representative dataset that accurately represents the range of topics and styles of conversation that the model will encounter.

▶ **Evaluation:** The performance of the AGI Chatbot can be evaluated using a variety of metrics, such as perplexity, BLEU score, and human evaluation. These metrics can be used to compare different models and to track the progress of a model as it's trained.

▶ **Use Cases:** The Artificial General Intelligence Chatbot has a number of potential use cases, including:
1. Engaging in natural language conversation with users, providing answers and insights on a variety of topics
2. Providing customer support and answering questions about products and services
3. Providing information and guidance to users, such as answering questions about health and wellness
4. Providing entertainment and entertainment-related information, such as answering questions about movies and TV shows

▶ **Limits and Risks:** Like any machine learning model, the AGI Chatbot has limitations and risks. One of the main limitations is that it may not always make accurate predictions, and may overlook important factors or make incorrect predictions about trustworthiness. Additionally, the model may be biased toward certain social behavior and online activities if the training data is not representative of the range of social and online information for the target population.

▶ **Common Myths or Misunderstandings:** There are a few common myths or misunderstandings about the AGI Chatbot. One myth is that the model can always generate accurate and appropriate responses, when in reality it can only provide a response based on the information it was trained on and may generate nonsensical, offensive, or misleading responses. Another myth is that the model can replace human conversation and understanding, when in reality it is intended to support and enhance human-like conversation and language understanding[33]. General intelligence tools suffer from many general problems, which is why I recommend only using them for creative endeavors, all of human knowledge drifts very rapidly, and it would be very hard for a model like this to unlearn past falsehoods, i.e. if the model was trained in 1400 it would say the world is flat, but then in 1493 it would probably still say the world is flat, even though the understanding of the truth had fundamentally changed.

▶ **Quality Grade:** B+

▶ **Cost to Create:** $100,000,000

▶ **Creator's Note:** AGI-type models like ChatGPT are very difficult to create but relatively easy to copy, models like this can give consistent "B+" answers to problems but probably will reach an upper limit on their ability to improve across varied domains, at which point a specific model should be trained.

5.3 Key Takeaways

▶ **Read the model cards.** As AI models become more sophisticated and widespread, it is essential to ensure that they are transparent and accountable. Model cards can help with this by providing information on the capabilities and limitations of AI models.

▶ **Avoid sucker traps.** There are several "sucker traps" to avoid when analyzing models, including inappropriately giving a model critical decision making ability, putting a model in a position where it needs to explain a particular decision, allowing a model to publish copyrighted material from its training data, and the ever-present concept drift the possibility of changes in the relationships in the training data, and the potential for biased training sets that can permanently shift the outputs of the model away from reality.

▶ **Understand the training data.** It is important to understand the data that is used to train a model and the domain in which it is deployed to forecast its strengths and weaknesses. Deep learning models are programmed not by a programmer, but by the data they are shown.

▶ **If you're unsure, allow the model to give low-stakes advice.** The more unsure you are about a particular model, the more effort you should put into managing it. In the very worst case you do not need to throw away all of your model's work, but instead allow it to participate as a non-voting member of your decision making committee, test your model and see how it performs with your supervision, some models should never be given decision making ability but can still be useful. More on this in the following chapters.

6

SELF-DRIVING WITH STATISTICS

"We think of automation as a machine doing a task that a human used to do...
you might think that means a human does nothing. But in fact there's abundant
literature that shows the human is not incurring no workload, the human is
now doing a different task and that task tends to be monitoring, a vigilance task,
looking for rare events...that is a task that humans are not well-equipped to do."
- Dr. Michael Nees, 2021 [34]

6.1 The Dangers of Semi-Autonomy

Two hundred years ago, horses were the most sophisticated mode of transportation. They possessed an innate ability to navigate terrain and avoid obstacles, even without a human rider at the reins. People often took comfort in the horse's natural instincts, which allowed for moments of respite during long journeys. Fast forward to today, where we have vehicles that claim to possess similar levels of autonomy, but with significantly more horsepower (pun intended).

One might be tempted to compare these self-driving cars to our trusty equine friends, imagining a world where vehicles, like horses, can be left to their own devices. Alas, this comparison is a misleading one, as it creates the illusion that our self-driving cars are more capable than they currently are.

The National Highway Traffic Safety Administration (NHTSA) has devised a six-level classification system to describe vehicle autonomy, ranging from Level 0 (no automation) to Level 5 (full automation). Most commercially available vehicles today hover between Levels 2 and 3, providing advanced driver assistance but requiring constant human oversight. This semi-autonomous state can lull drivers into a false sense of security, prompting them to disengage from the driving task in a manner that might have been acceptable during the days of horse-drawn carriages but is decidedly dangerous in the modern era.

In his book "Robot Take the Wheel," author Jason Torchinsky offers a compelling argument against semi- autonomy, dubbing it "stupid" in a section bearing the same name. Torchinsky highlights the impracticality of expecting a driver who has relinquished control to a semi-autonomous system to suddenly take over in a moment of crisis. Manufacturer warnings, while intended to encourage drivers to stay attentive, often go unheeded, creating a precarious situation where those behind the wheel are ill-prepared to intervene when the technology falters.[35]

The world of transportation extends beyond the realm of four-wheeled automobiles. The skies above host a veritable ballet of commercial aircraft, which rely on sophisticated autopilot systems to ferry passengers and cargo across vast distances. These systems differ in important ways from automobile autopilot and have significantly different infrastructure (not to mention terrain, or lack thereof). In aviation, autopilots demand constant monitoring and communication between the pilot, the aircraft, and air traffic control. In many ways, the intricacies and collaboration required for safe air travel can serve as a model for understanding the complexities of developing and implementing truly autonomous ground vehicles.

6.2   Comparing Autopilot Systems

At a glance, the autopilot systems in airplanes and Teslas may seem to share common goals: both strive to provide increased safety, efficiency, and convenience. However, the similarities largely end there, as the underlying technologies and the environments in which they operate diverge significantly.

Commercial airplanes, for example, are equipped with highly sophisticated autopilot systems capable of managing tasks such as altitude, speed, and heading control. In contrast, Tesla's advanced driver-assistance system (ADAS), while advanced, is focused primarily on lane keeping, adaptive cruise control, and collision avoidance. Furthermore, the aviation industry has a long history of integrating automation with well-established regulations, procedures, and training, whereas the automotive industry is still in the early stages of defining standards and best practices for autonomous vehicles.

One critical aspect of aircraft autopilot systems is the need for seamless communication and coordination with external systems, such as air traffic control (ATC) and other aircraft. This level of coordination ensures that each plane maintains a safe distance from others, follows established routes, and adheres to ATC instructions.

On the other hand, vehicles like Teslas currently have limited means of communication with external systems, relying instead on onboard sensors and mapping data to navigate the environment. As autonomous vehicle technology advances, however, it is anticipated that vehicle-to-vehicle (V2V) and vehicle-to-infrastructure (V2I) communication will become increasingly important for coordinating traffic flow and maintaining safety.

Despite the advanced nature of aircraft autopilot systems, pilots are still required to maintain a constant vigil, monitoring the system and intervening when necessary. This level of human oversight is not only mandated by regulations but also reinforced through rigorous training and the understanding that even the most advanced systems can fail.

In contrast, drivers of vehicles equipped with ADAS, such as Teslas, often face the temptation to over-rely on the technology and disengage from the driving task, as discussed in the previous section. This discrepancy highlights the need for clear guidelines and education on the proper use of semi-autonomous systems in cars, to ensure that drivers remain vigilant and prepared to intervene when needed.

6.3 Who Should The Car Kill?

In this section, we delve into the ethical dilemmas that arise when designing autonomous vehicles. We will discuss the Trolley Problem and its application to autonomous decision-making, as well as the legal and moral considerations of outsourcing responsibility to machines.

The Trolley Problem, a classic thought experiment in ethics, poses a hypothetical scenario where an individual must choose between two undesirable outcomes, often involving the deaths of different groups of people. In the context of autonomous vehicles, the Trolley Problem raises the question of how a self-driving car should prioritize the safety of its occupants, pedestrians, and other road users in situations where an accident is unavoidable.

As developers of autonomous vehicles grapple with these ethical quandaries, they must decide what values and priorities to embed in their algorithms. Should a self-driving car prioritize minimizing overall harm, protecting its passengers, or adhering to specific legal and moral rules? The choices made in designing these systems will have profound implications for society, as they will determine how autonomous vehicles respond in life-or-death situations.

The advent of autonomous vehicles raises complex questions about responsibility and liability. If a self-driving car is involved in an accident, who should be held accountable – the vehicle's owner, the manufacturer, or the software developer? As we outsource decision-making to machines, we must grapple with the legal and moral implications of this shift.

One potential approach is to establish a new legal framework that recognizes the unique nature of autonomous vehicles, assigning responsibility based on factors such as the level of autonomy, the specific circumstances of an accident, and the degree of human oversight. This would likely involve a combination of civil and criminal liability, as well as new insurance models to address the changing landscape of risk.

From a moral standpoint, the delegation of life-or-death decisions to machines raises profound questions about the nature of human agency and the limits of technological progress. As we continue to develop and deploy autonomous vehicles, it is crucial to engage in a broader societal conversation about the values and principles that should guide these advancements, ensuring that they serve the greater good while respecting individual rights and dignity.

The development of autonomous vehicles presents not only technological challenges but also complex ethical, legal, and moral dilemmas. By confronting these issues head-on, we can work toward a future where self-driving cars operate in harmony with human society, guided by shared values and a collective vision of progress.

6.4 Driving Infrastructure

As we delve deeper into the world of autonomous vehicles, it is essential to consider the broader infrastructure that supports these technologies. In this section, we will explore the challenges and opportunities related to maps, roads, sensors, software, and communications, shedding light on the complexities involved in creating a seamless, harmonious driving experience.

Maps play a crucial role in enabling autonomous vehicles to navigate their surroundings. However, one of the most significant challenges in map creation and maintenance is the concept drift – the ever-changing nature of our environments. Roads are altered, new construction projects arise, and traffic patterns shift. These changes can render maps outdated or inaccurate, as evidenced by the pileup crash cited in reference[36], where a self-driving car's reliance on outdated map data contributed to the accident.

Roads and urban design are equally important when considering the infrastructure necessary for self-driving cars. Retrofitting cities to accommodate autonomous vehicles may involve the creation of dedicated lanes, the installation of new traffic signals, and the adaptation of pedestrian spaces to ensure the safe coexistence of humans and machines. These changes will require collaboration between urban planners, transportation experts, and policymakers to ensure that cities evolve in a manner that supports the widespread adoption of self-driving cars.

Sensors are the eyes and ears of autonomous vehicles, allowing them to perceive and interpret their surroundings. However, these sensors are not infallible – they can be impaired by dirt, debris, and other environmental factors. A dirty sensor can compromise a self-driving car's ability to function safely, emphasizing the need for regular maintenance and cleaning to ensure optimal performance.

Software plays a central role in the operation of autonomous vehicles, and while you might think that this software is all proprietary, there are many completely open source platforms like OpenPilot [37] leading the way in developing advanced driver assistance systems. However, questions surrounding the inspection, regulation, and potential bankruptcy of software providers must be addressed. Additionally, the risk of software failures, as demonstrated in the over-the-air (OTA) crash cited in reference[38], highlights the need for robust safety mechanisms and regulatory oversight.

Finally, communication is a vital aspect of autonomous driving infrastructure. Autonomous vehicles must be capable of communicating not only with other cars but also with people, animals, and various elements of the environment. The emergence of new technologies and trends, such as vehicle-to-vehicle (V2V) and vehicle-to-infrastructure (V2I) communication, has the potential to revolutionize the way self-driving cars interact with their surroundings. However, these advances also bring new challenges in terms of privacy, security, and standardization.

The development and adoption of autonomous vehicles are not solely dependent on the cars themselves but also on the supporting infrastructure. By addressing the challenges and seizing the opportunities presented by maps, roads, sensors, software, and communications, we can work toward a future where self-driving cars and human-driven vehicles coexist harmoniously within a dynamic, evolving transportation ecosystem.

6.5 See You In Court!

As autonomous vehicles become more prevalent, it is inevitable that their integration into society will bring legal challenges and disputes. In this section, we will examine the complexities of multicollinearity and mathematical chaos, explainability and accountability in court, and the role of trustworthy machine learning and inherently interpretable models in addressing these challenges.

Multicollinearity and mathematical chaos introduce an element of uncertainty in the performance of autonomous vehicles. As multiple, highly correlated variables affect the behavior of self-driving cars, determining the cause of a specific event can be difficult. This problem is exacerbated by the chaotic nature of the systems involved, where small changes in initial conditions can lead to vastly different outcomes. These factors can make it challenging to attribute responsibility in the event of an accident, particularly when attempting to disentangle the contributions of various components, such as hardware, software, and environmental factors.

Explainability and accountability are critical concerns when presenting autonomous vehicle-related cases in court. If the decision-making processes of self-driving cars are inscrutable or difficult to understand, it becomes challenging to determine who or what is at fault in a given situation. This lack of transparency can impede the legal process and erode public trust in autonomous vehicle technology.

One potential solution to these challenges is the development of trustworthy machine learning, as described in Trustworthy ML[39]. By teaching developers to build models that are reliable, interpretable, and robust, we can create autonomous vehicles that are more easily understood and evaluated in legal proceedings. This approach prioritizes transparency and accountability, ensuring that the underlying algorithms driving these vehicles can be scrutinized and their decisions explained.

In order to achieve explainability in artificial intelligence, it may be necessary to reconsider the recent advancements in deep neural networks.

While these networks have demonstrated impressive performance, their opacity can make it difficult to understand how decisions are being made. This is where less advanced technology may have an advantage, as it allows for more transparency in the decision-making process. However, even with less advanced models such as decision trees, there is still the potential for complexity to create challenges in explainability. While theoretically fully explainable, decision trees can become cumbersome when they contain millions of lines of rules or code. As a result, they can be just as difficult to explain in a court of law as more advanced neural networks.

Inherently interpretable models further reinforce the case for transparency and accountability in autonomous vehicles. By developing machine learning models that are not only accurate but also readily interpretable, we can facilitate a more straightforward assessment of responsibility in the event of an accident. This clarity can help build public trust in the technology while also streamlining the legal process when disputes arise.

6.6   Alternative Approaches

As we explore the future of autonomous vehicles, it is crucial to consider alternative ways of thinking about self-driving cars and their potential roles in our transportation ecosystem. In this section, we will discuss various concepts that challenge conventional notions of autonomy and offer novel solutions that could complement or transform our understanding of mobility.

One alternative approach involves reimagining self-driving cars as a form of "train" that operates in dedicated lanes. By constructing special lanes for autonomous vehicles, we can essentially put these cars "on rails," enabling them to function more like a train. This approach would not only enhance the safety and efficiency of autonomous vehicles but also provide a glimpse into the potential infrastructural and regulatory frameworks necessary for their success.

In the realm of logistics and warehousing, the lack of self-driving forklifts offers an interesting lesson. Instead of focusing on automating forklifts, warehouses have implemented moving shelves, essentially flipping the problem on its head to achieve a more efficient solution. This example highlights the importance of rethinking traditional approaches to autonomy and searching for innovative ways to streamline various aspects of our economy.

Building on these ideas, we can explore other unconventional approaches that challenge the status quo of autonomous vehicles. One possibility is the development of platooning systems, in which multiple vehicles travel in close proximity, communicating with one another to maintain safety and optimize traffic flow. This approach could harness the advantages of vehicle-to-vehicle communication while reducing the need for extensive infrastructure modifications.

Another alternative is the concept of supervised autonomy, not from the driver at a moment's notice like we have today, but from a control tower similar to those used at airports. This has large privacy implications but combines the benefits of autonomous technology with human oversight. This approach allows for human intervention in complex or high-risk situations, mitigating concerns about delegating life-or-death decisions to machines while still reaping the rewards of autonomous driving.

In all these alternative approaches, the key is to think creatively about how we can integrate self-driving cars into our transportation systems. By challenging conventional wisdom and exploring innovative solutions, we can create a more efficient, sustainable, and harmonious future for transportation, one that redefines the role of autonomous vehicles within an ever-evolving paradigm.

6.7 Key Takeaways

▶ **Redefine autonomy with alternative approaches:** Consider dedicated lanes, supervised autonomy, and other unconventional methods to enhance safety and efficiency while reimagining the role of self-driving cars in our transportation systems.

▶ **Adapt to ever-changing driving infrastructure:** Address challenges in maps, roads, sensors, software, and communications to create a seamless, harmonious driving experience, while ensuring regular maintenance and updates. Embrace open-source software and standardized solutions to foster collaboration and innovation.

▶ **Prioritize explainability and accountability:** Develop trustworthy machine learning and inherently interpretable models to enhance transparency, facilitate legal proceedings, and build public trust in autonomous vehicle technology.

▶ **Leverage communication and collaboration:** Promote vehicle-to-vehicle communication, coordination with external systems, and remote control for improved safety, efficiency, and adaptability in a dynamic transportation environment. Encourage the adoption of industry standards to facilitate interoperability and streamline implementation.

▶ **Balance innovation with regulation:** Establish robust regulatory frameworks that protect privacy, maintain accountability, and ensure safety while fostering technological advancements, and integrating autonomous vehicles into our evolving transportation landscape.

7

UNPLUGGING SKYNET

"The second requirement of goal-misalignment risk is that an intelligent machine can commandeer the Earth's resources to pursue its goals, or in other ways prevent us from stopping it... We have similar concerns with humans. This is why no single person or entity can control the entire internet and why we require multiple people to launch a nuclear missile. Intelligent machines will not develop misaligned goals unless we go to great lengths to endow them with that ability. Even if they did, no machine can commandeer the world's resources unless we let it. We don't let a single human, or even a small number of humans, control the world's resources. We need to be similarly careful with machines."
- Jeff Hawkins, 2022[15]

7.1 Landmines Everywhere

As we explore the potential of artificial intelligence in the realm of warfare, it is crucial to approach the topic of autonomous weapons with a healthy dose of skepticism. To fully grasp the inherent risks of these weapons, we need look no further than the history of landmines. These indiscriminate, uncontrollable devices should serve as a stark reminder of the potential pitfalls associated with the development and deployment of autonomous weaponry.

Landmines have long been a staple of military strategy, yet their consequences continue to plague countless communities around the world. Once deployed, landmines cannot differentiate between friend or foe, soldier or civilian. They lie dormant, waiting to unleash their destructive force on unsuspecting victims, often long after the conflict has ceased. This lack of control and the resulting collateral damage make landmines a morally and ethically questionable choice in modern warfare.

When examining the prospect of advanced AI-powered autonomous weapons, we must confront the reality that these systems may ultimately share the same fundamental flaw as landmines: the lack of control. While it is true that AI technology has the potential to drastically reduce human casualties and improve targeting precision, it is crucial to recognize the potential for these weapons to become indiscriminate and uncontrollable, much like their landmine predecessors. Once released into the world, these autonomous systems may wreak havoc beyond their intended targets and pose a significant threat to innocent lives.

The dystopian vision of a "Skynet" scenario, as popularized by the Terminator series, should remain firmly in the realm of science fiction. It is not only an unrealistic portrayal of AI development but also a dangerously misguided idea to pursue. Instead of fixating on a sensationalized and unlikely outcome, we must focus our attention on understanding the true consequences and ethical implications of AI-powered weaponry. We must recognize that creating uncontrollable, indiscriminate weapons is neither wise nor responsible.

As we venture further into the domain of AI and autonomous weapons, let us heed the lessons from landmines and strive to build a future where technology serves to protect and preserve, rather than to destroy indiscriminately. By approaching this complex issue with an informed and critical perspective, we can work together to ensure that the perils of the past are not repeated and that we create a more conscientious and responsible future for AI-powered warfare.

7.2 The Autonomous Weapons Fallacy

The development of AI-driven autonomous weapons raises ethical and practical concerns. One such concern is the potential for AI to gain complete control over these weapons systems, a fear that is often exaggerated and misplaced. In reality, there is a concept called "useful incompatibility," which is built into many systems to prevent any single entity from assuming total control. This incompatibility is crucial for maintaining security and integrity in our increasingly interconnected world.

AI systems would face immense challenges in attempting to operate across diverse platforms, interfaces, and protocols. These systems would need to be able to manipulate physical keys, communicate with humans, and navigate different operating systems, among other complex tasks. This "useful incompatibility" serves as a safeguard to ensure that AI cannot unilaterally commandeer autonomous weapons or any other critical systems.

Debunking the myth of uncontrolled AI requires a clearer understanding of the nature of intelligence. Yann LeCun's article[1] offers a valuable perspective on this topic:

> "We dramatically overestimate the threat of an accidental AI takeover, because we tend to conflate intelligence with the drive to achieve dominance. [...] Intelligence does not provide the goal itself, merely the means to achieve it. 'Natural intelligence'—the intelligence of biological organisms—is an evolutionary adaptation, and like other such adaptations, it emerged under natural selection because it improved survival and propagation of the species."

Unfortunately, many experts in the field seem to misunderstand this crucial distinction. For example, Jon Krohn's TED talk ends with a scary side note that if AI becomes slightly more intelligent than humans, it could dominate us in the same way that humans have dominated apes[40]. This argument, however, is fundamentally flawed. The mere possession of greater strength, speed, or intelligence does not automatically lead to dominance or obsolescence. A construction machine's ability to lift 100 times more than a human does not make it our master, just as AI's capability to synthesize text or solve mathematical problems at a faster pace than us does not render humanity obsolete.

The notion that AI could simply outpace and overpower humanity is rooted in a narrow understanding of intelligence and power dynamics. This perspective is sometimes promoted by prominent figures in the tech industry, leading to misconceptions and undue fear. As we continue to explore the potential of AI and autonomous weapons, it is vital to approach these topics with nuance and a deep understanding of the underlying principles. Only then can we engage in a meaningful and informed conversation about the future of AI and its potential impact on our world.

7.3 Where's the Off Button?

Asimov's Three Laws of Robotics have captivated the imagination of science fiction enthusiasts and AI researchers alike. However, upon closer examination, it becomes apparent that these laws may not be as robust or practical as they first appear. In particular, the third law raises concerns about the necessity and implications of imbuing AI with self-preservation instincts.

Asimov's Three Laws of Robotics are as follows:

- *First Law: A robot may not injure a human being or, through inaction, allow a human being to come to harm.*

- *Second Law: A robot must obey the orders given it by human beings except where such orders would conflict with the First Law.*

- *Third Law: A robot must protect its own existence as long as such protection does not conflict with the First or Second Law.*

One crucial aspect to consider when evaluating the practicality of Asimov's laws is the concept of consent. Human beings have the right to make decisions about their own safety and well-being, even if those decisions may carry risks. By strictly adhering to the First Law, AI systems may inadvertently undermine human autonomy and choice, leading to a paternalistic relationship between AI and its human users. It is essential that AI systems are designed to respect and prioritize human consent, ensuring that individual autonomy is preserved.

The Third Law, which requires a robot to protect its own existence, introduces an unnecessary and potentially problematic element of self-preservation. In the realm of AI and robotics, it is crucial that these systems have a built-in mechanism to shut down or be controlled when necessary. In this context, an "off button" serves as a vital safety measure, allowing human operators to intervene and regain control over a potentially malfunctioning or misaligned AI system.

Asimov's Third Law, by prioritizing the protection of a robot's existence, inadvertently creates the potential for conflict between the AI and its human operators. Security by obscurity can be a valuable approach to ensure that AI systems remain under human control, preventing the possibility of AI systems becoming dangerous or adversarial.

7.4 You Can't Handle The Truth!

Deep learning systems, which form the backbone of many AI applications, are notoriously difficult to interpret. As these systems become more complex and integrated into various aspects of our lives, the need for transparency and interpretability becomes increasingly crucial. The legal and ethical implications of AI actions can be challenging to navigate, particularly in high-stakes environments such as warfare[41].

Consider, for example, the difficulties faced in explaining a self-driving car's actions in court. The problem becomes even more daunting when trying to justify the decisions made by an autonomous weapon. Without a clear understanding of the underlying logic and decision-making processes, the consequences of AI-driven actions may lead to ethical dilemmas and questions of accountability.

Machine learning models are only as good as the data they are trained on. Biased training data can lead to biased outcomes, which can have far-reaching consequences, particularly in the context of autonomous weapons. Moreover, the nature of threats and warfare is constantly evolving. This concept drift makes it difficult for AI systems to adapt to new situations and can be exploited by adversaries to gain an advantage.

The dynamic and ever-changing landscape of warfare necessitates AI systems capable of learning and adapting in real-time. Failure to address the challenges posed by concept drift and biased training data can lead to suboptimal decision-making and the potential for unintended harm.

AI systems, particularly those used in warfare, may be vulnerable to adversarial attacks. These attacks can exploit weaknesses in the AI's algorithms, causing the system to behave in unpredictable or undesirable ways. In some cases, adversarial attacks could even turn an AI system against its creators.

Imagine a scenario in which an adversarial nation-state discovers a weakness in an AI-powered reconnaissance drone. By exploiting this vulnerability, they are able to manipulate the drone's AI, causing it to transmit false intelligence or even engage in hostile actions against friendly forces. The consequences of such an event could be disastrous, undermining trust in AI systems and potentially escalating conflicts.

As we continue to develop and deploy AI-driven systems in the context of warfare, it is essential to address the challenges of interpretability, transparency, biased training data, and vulnerability to adversarial attacks. By doing so, we can ensure that AI serves as a force for good, enhancing our ability to protect and defend ourselves while minimizing the risks of unintended harm.

7.5 AI Doesn't Kill People, People Kill People

"First World War was known as 'the war to end all wars,' although some historians now argue it didn't. But it was the first high-tech war, with aeroplanes, machine guns and tanks all rising up to fight the human beings that made them. Despite having no beliefs or ideology or hearts or souls, the killing machines were victorious. The final score was weaponry 20 million, mankind nil."
Cunk On Earth Season 1 Episode 3[42]

The discourse surrounding AI in warfare often tends to be imprecise and misleading, resulting in a distorted understanding of the role artificial intelligence plays in modern conflict. AI-powered tools may indeed enhance military capabilities, but it is crucial to recognize that these weapons are AI-enabled, not autonomous. They operate under human command and control, serving as an extension of human decision-making rather than as independent actors [43].

To attribute blame or responsibility to AI in the context of warfare is to fundamentally misunderstand the nature of these systems. Artificial intelligence is a tool, one that can be wielded by human beings for various purposes, both benign and malicious. Just as a hammer can be used to build or destroy, AI can be employed to improve lives or inflict harm. The key determinant in each scenario is the intent and actions of the person wielding the tool, not the tool itself.

In our pursuit of technological advancements and AI-driven military capabilities, it is essential to maintain a clear and accurate understanding of the relationship between human actors and the tools they employ. By doing so, we can foster a more informed and nuanced conversation about the role of AI in warfare and the ethical implications that come with its use.

As we continue to develop and deploy AI-enabled weapons, let us never lose sight of the fact that it is ultimately people who make the decisions and bear the responsibility for their consequences. It is our collective responsibility to ensure that we use AI ethically, responsibly, and in the service of peace, rather than allowing it to become a mere instrument of destruction.

7.6 Key Takeaways

- **Autonomous weapons are not self-determined** AI-enabled weapons require human oversight and control, emphasizing that the responsibility for their use and consequences lies with human decision-makers.

- **Intelligence does not equate to a drive for dominance** AI systems are tools designed to acquire and apply knowledge in pursuit of a goal, but the goal itself is determined by human actors, not the AI.

- **Asimov's Third Law is flawed** AI systems need an off button and should not be designed to prioritize their own preservation over ethical considerations.

- **Transparency and interpretability are crucial** The challenges of understanding AI systems' decision- making processes must be addressed to ensure accountability and ethical use in warfare.

- **Address biases, concept drift, and adversarial attacks** Ensuring that AI-driven systems are robust, adaptable, and free of biases is essential for their responsible and effective deployment in the context of warfare.

8

REVOLUTIONARY FOR WHOM?

"The inhabitant of London could order by telephone, sipping his morning tea in bed, the various products of the whole earth – he could at the same time and by the same means adventure his wealth in the natural resources and new enterprise of any quarter of the world – he could secure forthwith, if he wished, cheap and comfortable means of transit to any country or climate without passport or other formality."
- John Maynard Keynes, 1920 [44]

8.1 Assistance from Assistants

"Living off the wits of his subordinates - maybe that's leadership these days" [45]

You know, the whole concept of having an assistant has changed quite a bit over the years. In the old days, a well-to-do family might have employed a butler to help manage their estate, while nowadays, folks can simply use digital assistants like Siri or ChatGPT. But that's not all! There's also an interesting hybrid of sorts that has emerged in recent times – the Indian Virtual Assistant.

Now, if you think about it, traditional butlers were a sort of luxury. They cost a pretty penny and were thus reserved for the upper crust of society. On the other hand, these digital assistants – Siri, ChatGPT, and the like –

well, they're pretty affordable, and just about anyone with a smartphone can access them. In a way, they've democratized assistance.

But there's another option that lies somewhere in between: the Indian Virtual Assistant. These human assistants, often based in India, provide remote support at a fraction of the cost of an in-person butler. They offer the human touch that digital assistants can't quite replicate, while still maintaining a certain level of affordability.

Now, don't get me wrong – I'm not saying digital assistants are bad. They're incredibly useful! But they've got some drawbacks, too. One concern is the potential for hacking and bugs. These AI-driven helpers are connected to the internet, and that means some folks with malicious intentions might try to break in and steal sensitive data. Plus, as impressive as machine learning can be, it's not perfect. Sometimes, these digital assistants might give you an answer that's a bit... off.

So, who might steer clear of AI assistants, despite their affordability and widespread availability? Well, for one, there are people who value their privacy and would rather not have a potential security risk handling their affairs. Then there are those who simply find comfort in human interaction, even if it means shelling out a little extra for a human assistant.

At the end of the day, the world of assistance has seen quite a revolution. As we navigate this new landscape, it's important to think about the trade-offs between cost, convenience, security, and the value of human expertise in the age of artificial intelligence.

8.2 The Limitations of AI-generated Content

> *"Another definition of modernity: conversations can be more and*
> *more completely reconstructed with clips from other conversations*
> *taking place at the same time on the planet.", "You are alive in inverse*
> *proportion to the density of cliches in your writing."*[23]

When it comes to AI-generated content, there's a certain fascination with the way machines can replicate human-like conversations. But are these AI-generated conversations truly akin to the ones between humans? Well, not exactly.

Let's take ChatGPT as an example. A recent article described it as a "Blurry JPEG of the Web" [12], and that's quite an apt description. While AI models like ChatGPT are capable of generating coherent and contextually relevant responses, they often lack the depth and originality that genuine human conversations possess. In essence, AI-generated content can sometimes feel like a collage of borrowed ideas and phrases, strung together to mimic a conversation, but lacking the unique perspective and spontaneity that real human interaction entails.

Now, if we compare AI-generated content to traditional search engines, we can see some interesting differences. A search engine retrieves information from the vast expanse of the internet, presenting it to the user for their interpretation. An AI like ChatGPT, on the other hand, processes and generates content using a sophisticated regression model. But here's the catch: it might not always be right.

"(Traditional) search engines are databases, organized collections of data that can be stored, updated, and retrieved at will. (Traditional) search engines are indexes. a form of database, that connect things like keywords to URLs; they can be swiftly updated, incrementally, bit by bit (as when you update a phone number in the database that holds your contacts).

Large language models do something very different: they are not databases; they are text predictors, turbocharged versions of autocomplete. Fundamentally, what they learn are relationships between bits of text, like words, phrases, even whole sentences. And they use those relationships to predict other bits of text. And then they do something almost magical: they paraphrase those bits of texts, almost like a thesaurus but much much better. But as they do so, as they glom stuff together, something often gets lost in

translation: which bits of text do and do not truly belong together."
Gary Marcus, 2023 [46]

In this sense, AI-generated content can be thought of as a creative interpretation of the information available to it. While it can provide valuable insights and answers, its limitations stem from its inability to truly comprehend the nuances of human conversation and thought. Consequently, the content produced may occasionally fall short in terms of accuracy, authenticity, or originality.

Therefore, as we continue to integrate AI-generated content into our lives, it's crucial to remember that these AI models, while impressive, are not perfect. They can offer valuable assistance, but they should not be treated as infallible sources of information or as substitutes for genuine human interaction.

8.3 The AI Advantage in the Workplace

There's a long-standing belief that human intelligence is unrivaled, and while it's true that humans possess unique capabilities, it's important to recognize the immense value AI can bring to the workplace.

Consider the humble calculator, for instance. Before its invention, humans would manually perform complex calculations, a process that was not only time-consuming but also prone to errors. The introduction of calculators transformed the way we approached mathematics, allowing us to quickly and accurately solve problems. Similarly, AI has the potential to revolutionize the way we work by handling tasks that would otherwise require significant time and effort from humans.

By embracing AI in daily tasks and careers, we can delegate responsibilities that computers excel at, such as processing large datasets, pattern recognition, and even language translation. This not only improves efficiency and accuracy but also frees up human workers to focus on tasks that require creativity, empathy, and critical thinking – areas where AI still falls short.

The key to reaping the benefits of AI in the workplace lies in finding the right balance between human expertise and AI capabilities. Rather than viewing AI as a threat to human intelligence, we should approach it as a powerful tool that complements and enhances our own skills. By working in tandem with AI, we can unlock new levels of productivity, innovation, and growth.

Ultimately, the integration of AI into the workplace offers countless opportunities for both individuals and organizations to thrive. By challenging the notion of superior human intelligence and acknowledging the strengths of AI, we can forge a harmonious partnership that drives success in the ever-evolving world of business.

8.4 The "Organic Content" Market

As AI becomes increasingly prevalent in content production, we may witness the emergence of a new market segment: handcrafted, 100% organic content that is AI-free. This trend would be akin to the demand for organic, artisanal products in other industries, where consumers seek authenticity and the human touch.

The appeal of organic content lies in its perceived originality, creativity, and the assurance that it is the result of genuine human effort. This type of content may be highly sought after in industries such as journalism, literature, and the arts, where the value of human expression and unique perspectives are paramount.

However, the rise of this market also brings with it the potential for fraud. As AI-generated content becomes increasingly sophisticated and indistinguishable from human-generated content, distinguishing between the two may become a significant challenge. Unscrupulous individuals may attempt to pass off AI-generated content as organic, capitalizing on the demand for authentic human creations.

In order to combat fraud in the organic content market, it will be crucial to develop reliable methods for verifying the authenticity of content. This could include the use of digital signatures, blockchain technology, or other innovative solutions that provide a clear and tamper-proof record of a content's origin.

Moreover, fostering a culture of transparency and accountability within the content creation industry will be essential. By setting high ethical standards and encouraging open communication about the use of AI in content production, both creators and consumers can work together to ensure that the value of genuine human expression is preserved and celebrated.

8.5   A Framework for Navigating AI's Impact on Careers

In order to effectively navigate the impact of AI on careers, it is essential to develop a comprehensive framework that addresses the challenges and opportunities that arise from this technological revolution. The following framework can help navigate AI's impact on your business and career.

8.5.1 *Assess the Landscape*

a. Identify AI-affected tasks: Analyze your industry and job function to pinpoint tasks that are most likely to be influenced by AI. Consider which tasks are repetitive, data-intensive, or involve pattern recognition, as these are prime candidates for AI-driven automation.

b. Evaluate AI maturity: Assess the maturity of AI technologies relevant to your field, taking into account their current capabilities and potential future developments. This will help you gauge the timeline for AI adoption and its impact on job functions.

8.5.2 *Embrace AI as a Collaborator*

a. Leverage AI for productivity: Identify areas where AI can enhance your productivity by automating routine tasks, streamlining processes, or augmenting decision-making. Embrace AI as a tool that complements your skills and expertise, rather than a competitor.

b. Cultivate human-centric skills: Focus on developing skills that are uniquely human, such as creativity, empathy, critical thinking, and communication. These skills will remain valuable in the job market, even as AI becomes more pervasive.

8.5.3 *Adapt and Upskill*

a. Pursue continuous learning: Stay abreast of the latest AI advancements and their implications for your industry. Engage in lifelong learning through professional development courses, workshops, and industry events to maintain your competitiveness in the job market.

b. Acquire AI-related skills: Gain proficiency in AI-related skills, such as data analysis, machine learning, programming, or AI ethics. This will enable you to better understand and navigate the AI landscape, making you a more valuable asset to your organization.

8.5.4 *Shape the Future of Work*

a. Advocate for responsible AI adoption: Promote ethical AI implementation within your organization, addressing issues such as fairness, accountability, transparency, and privacy. Encourage the development of AI solutions that augment human capabilities, rather than replace them.

b. Champion workforce transformation: Support initiatives that facilitate workforce adaptation to AI, such as reskilling programs, mentorship opportunities, and the creation of new roles that leverage both human and AI strengths.

By following this framework, professionals can effectively navigate the impact of AI on their careers, seizing opportunities for growth and ensuring their continued success in the rapidly evolving world of work.

8.6   Dead Inside

> *"If you know, in the morning, what your day looks like with any precision you are a little bit dead - the more precision the more dead you are."*[23]

Conversational regression, or the tendency for AI-generated content to be a mere rehashing of existing ideas and phrases, can indeed result in rather monotonous and derivative interactions. In this sense, AI is, metaphorically speaking, "dead inside," lacking the spontaneity, creativity, and emotional depth that define human conversations.

While AI-powered tools like ChatGPT are impressive in their ability to generate coherent and contextually relevant responses, they cannot truly replicate the unique spark that arises from genuine human interaction. This is where we, as humans, can reclaim our strengths and embrace the richness of our own personalities and experiences.

Instead of attempting to imbue AI with the same emotional and intellectual depth as humans, we can leverage its strengths in areas such as data processing, pattern recognition, and automation, while focusing on cultivating our own unique skills and attributes. This approach allows us to maximize the potential of both AI and humans, enabling each to thrive in their respective domains.

So, let us embrace AI for what it is - a powerful tool that can enhance our lives and free us from mundane tasks. By doing so, we can devote more time and energy to the pursuits that make us truly human, be it creative endeavors, fostering deep connections with others, or simply exploring the world around us with curiosity and wonder.

In this way, we can create a harmonious balance between humans and AI, ensuring that we complement each other's strengths while preserving the very essence of what makes us alive.

8.7   Go Forth and Procreate, Let The Calculators Multiply!

To close, I will address some concerns raised in an open letter signed by Elon Musk and Steve Wozniak in 2023. [47]

8.7.1 *Should we let machines flood our information channels with propaganda and untruth?*

The issue of propaganda and untruth in our information channels is not unique to AI-generated content. It is already a problem with state actors and other entities manipulating information. The solution lies in promoting media literacy and encouraging individuals to seek reputable news sources, such as the New York Times or the Wall Street Journal, rather than relying solely on social media for their information.

8.7.2 *Should we automate away all the jobs, including the fulfilling ones?*

Automation is a natural progression of technology, and it is impossible to regulate it away. If people find fulfillment in tasks that are automatable, they can still engage in these activities as hobbies or artisanal crafts. For example, they could open an Etsy shop and handcraft their products, or sharpen pencils by hand. Embracing AI and automation allows us to focus on more fulfilling, creative, and intellectually stimulating tasks that are uniquely human.

8.7.3 *Should we develop nonhuman minds that might eventually outnumber, outsmart, obsolete and replace us?*

The fear of AI outsmarting or replacing humans is based on the flawed assumption that being better at a single task implies complete superiority. AI systems may excel in specific domains, such as scoring high on standardized tests, but this does not mean they can replace humans altogether. The argument that AI will replace humans in the same way humans "replaced" our ape ancestors is misguided, as AI lacks the biological drive to procreate and compete. It is important to recognize that AI systems are tools designed to complement human abilities, not rivals seeking to supplant us.

8.7.4 *Should we risk loss of control of our civilization?*

The notion of "losing control" of our civilization is a vague and misguided concern. Civilization is not a monolithic entity controlled by a single puppeteer but rather a complex, evolving system driven by the collective actions of individuals, communities, and institutions. Embracing AI does not mean relinquishing control over our society; instead, it provides us with powerful tools to shape our world and address the challenges we face. By integrating AI responsibly and ethically, we can harness its potential for the betterment of our civilization.

8.8   Key Takeaways

- **AI assistants aren't as good as butlers, but they are much cheaper** AI assistants, like ChatGPT and Siri, provide cost-effective and efficient alternatives to traditional butlers and virtual assistants, but users must consider potential drawbacks such as hackability and bugs.

- **AI-generated content has limitations** While AI can produce content quickly and efficiently, it may lack the authenticity and depth of human-generated content, leading to a rise in the "organic content" market.

▶ **Embrace AI in the workplace** AI tools can enhance productivity and allow humans to focus on more creative and intellectually stimulating tasks, similar to how calculators have transformed mathematical work.

▶ **AI's "dead inside" nature** AI systems may be proficient at specific tasks, but they lack the human touch and personality, making it crucial for humans to focus on what we do best.

▶ **Debunking AI misconceptions** AI is not a rival seeking to replace humans; instead, it is a powerful tool designed to complement human abilities and help shape our world.

BIBLIOGRAPHY

Here are the references in citation order.

1   Yann LeCun Anthony Zador. *Don't Fear the Terminator - Scientific American Blog Network*. https://blogs.scientificamerican.com/observations/dont-fear-the-terminator/. Sept. 2019 (cited on pages 17, 133).

2   The Economist. *A battle royal is brewing over copyright and AI*. https://www.economist.com/business/ 2023/03/15/a-battle-royal-is-brewing-over-copyright-and-ai. Mar. 2023 (cited on page 18).

3   Stephen O'Grady. *The Software Paradox*. en. Sebastopol, CA: O'Reilly Media, July 2015 (cited on page 19).

4   Marc Andreesen. *Why AI Won't Cause Unemployment*. https://pmarca.substack.com/p/why-ai-wont-cause-unemployment. Mar. 2023 (cited on page 20).

5   Cecilia Kang and Adam Satariano. *As A.I. Booms, Lawmakers Struggle to Understand the Technology*. https://www.nytimes.com/2023/03/03/technology/artificial-intelligence-regulation-congress.html. Mar. 2023 (cited on page 20).

6   Morning Consult. *Generative AI Wins Some Early Fans But Is Missing Public Trust*. https://morningconsult.com/2023/02/22/generative-ai-fans-public-trust/. Feb. 2023 (cited on page 20).

7   Monmouth University. *Artificial Intelligence Use Prompts Concerns*. https://www.monmouth.edu/polling-institute/reports/monmouthpoll us 021523/. Feb. 2023 (cited on page 20).

8   Blake Lemoine. *'I Worked on Google's AI. My Fears Are Coming True'*. https://www.newsweek.com/google- ai-blake-lemoine-bing-chatbot-sentient-1783340. Feb. 2023 (cited on page 20).

9   Ethan Mollick. *Secret Cyborgs: The Present Disruption in Three Papers*. https://oneusefulthing.substack.com/p/secret-cyborgs-the-present-disruption. Mar. 2023 (cited on page 22).

10   Joshua Needelman. *Forget Utopia. Ignore Dystopia. Embrace Protopia!* https://www. nytimes.com/2023/03/14/special-series/protopia-movement.html. Mar. 2023 (cited on page 22).

11   The Economist. *Lessons from finance's experience with artificial intelligence.* https:// www.economist.com/finance-and-economics/2023/03/09/lessons-from-finances-experience-with-artificial-intelligence. 2023 (cited on page 22).

12   Ted Chiang. *ChatGPT Is a Blurry JPEG of the Web.* https:// www. newyorker. com/ tech/ annals- of- technology/chatgpt-is-a-blurry-jpeg-of-the-web. 2023 (cited on pages 23, 141).

13   Matt Welsh. *The end of programming.* Jan. 2023. url: https://cacm.acm.org/ magazines/2023/1/267976- the-end-of-programming/fulltext (cited on page 27).

14   Elaine Rich, Kevin Knight, and Shivashankar B. Nair. *Artificial Intelligence.* Tata McGraw-Hill, 2009 (cited on page 28).

15   Jeff Hawkins. *A thousand brains: A new theory of intelligence.* Basic Books, 2022 (cited on pages 35, 131).

16   Caglar Aytekin. 'Neural Networks are Decision Trees'. In: (2022). doi: 10.48550/ ARXIV.2210.05189 (cited on page 37).

17   Francois Chollet. *Deep learning with python, second edition.* Manning Publications, 2022 (cited on pages 44, 46).

18   Brian Christian. *The Alignment Problem: Machine Learning and Human Values.* W. W. Norton & Company, 2020 (cited on page 57).

19   Nicholas Carlini et al. *Extracting Training Data from Diffusion Models.* 2023. doi: 10.48550/ARXIV.2301.13188. url: https://arxiv.org/abs/2301.13188 (cited on page 60).

20   Kyle Barr. *Getty Images Claims Stable Diffusion's Creator 'Copied' 12 Million Copyrighted Images.* https://news.yahoo.com/getty-images-claims-stable-diffusions-220000016.html. Feb. 2023 (cited on page 60).

21   Garry Kasparov. *Ai should augment human intelligence, not replace it: Harvard Business Review: March 18, 2021.* Mar. 2021. url: https://www.kasparov.com/ai-should-augment-human-intelligence-not-replace-it-harvard-business-review-march-18-2021/ (cited on page 61).

22   Vikram Mansharamani. *Think for yourself: Restoring common sense in an age of experts and artificial intelligence.* Harvard Business Review Press, 2020 (cited on page 62).

23   Nassim Nicholas Taleb. *The bed of Procrustes.* Incerto. Random House Trade, Oct. 2016 (cited on pages 66, 140, 146).

24   Benj Edwards. *New Go-playing trick defeats world-class Go AI—but loses to human amateurs | Ars Technica.* https://arstechnica.com/information-technology/2022/11/

new-go-playing-trick-defeats-world-class-go-ai-but-loses-to-human-amateurs/. Nov. 2022 (cited on page 77).

25   Nicola Davis. *AI skin cancer diagnoses risk being less accurate for dark skin – study.* https://www.theguardian.com/society/2021/nov/09/ai-skin-cancer- diagnoses-risk-being-less-accurate-for-dark-skin-study. Nov. 2021 (cited on page 86).

26   *Overturning Wrongful Convictions Involving Misapplied Forensics.* https:// innocenceproject.org/misapplication-of-forensic-science/. Feb. 2023 (cited on page 89).

27   Cami Rosso. *AI Finds Drug Candidate for Liver Cancer in 30 Days | Psychology Today.* https://www.psychologytoday.com/us/blog/the-future-brain/202301/ai-finds-drug-candidate-for-liver-cancer-in-30-days. Jan. 2023 (cited on page 91).

28   Karen Weintraub. *New algorithm detects autism in infants. How might that change care?* https://www.usatoday.com/story/news/health/2023/02/08/autism-signs-early-life-study/11164013002/. Feb. 2023 (cited on page 93).

29   Lucas Nolan. *Joe Biden Releases Executive Order Promoting Woke AI.* https://www. breitbart.com/tech/2023/02/22/joe- biden-releases-executive-order-promoting-woke-ai/. Feb. 2023 (cited on page 101).

30   Adam Satariano and Mike Isaac. *The Silent Partner Cleaning Up Facebook for 500 Million a Year.* https://www.nytimes.com/2021/08/31/technology/facebook-accenture-content-moderation.html. 2021 (cited on page 101).

31   Matt Richtel. *Why Apple Watches Keep Calling 911 - The New York Times.* https:// www.nytimes.com/2023/02/03/health/apple-watch-911-emergency-call.html. Feb. 2023 (cited on page 109).

32   Adrianna Nine. *US Marines Defeat DARPA Robot by Hiding Under a Cardboard Box - ExtremeTech.* https://www.extremetech.com/extreme/342413-us-marines-defeat-darpa-robot-by-hiding-under-a-cardboard-box. Jan. 2023 (cited on page 111).

33   Josh A. Goldstienen. *Forecasting Potential Misuses of Language Models for Disinformation Campaigns—and How to Reduce Risk.* https://openai.com/blog/forecasting-misuse/. Jan. 2023 (cited on page 119).

34   PAVE Virtual Panel. *"When Humans Meet Automation: What the Research Tells Us".* https://www.youtube.com/watch?v=45mJGYiqrxY. July 2020 (cited on page 121).

35   Jason Torchinsky and Beau Boeckmann. *Robot, take the wheel: The road to autonomous cars and the lost art of driving.* Apollo Publishers, 2019 (cited on page 122).

36   Jason Torchinsky. *Newly Released Video Of Thanksgiving Day Tesla Full Self-Driving Crash Demonstrates The Fundamental Problem Of Semi-Automated Driving Systems.* https://www.theautopian.com/newly-released-video-of-thanksgiving-day-

tesla-full-self-driving-crash-demonstrates-the-fundamental-problem-of-semi-automated-driving-systems/. 2022 (cited on page 125).

37   OpenPilot Team. *GitHub - commaai/openpilot: openpilot is an open source driver assistance system. openpilot performs the functions of Automated Lane Centering and Adaptive Cruise Control for over 200 supported car makes and models.* https://github.com/commaai/openpilot. 2023 (cited on page 126).

38   Tom Krishner Nick Lichtenberg and The Associated Press. *Tesla recalls all 362,758 vehicles with Full Self-Driving Beta because it 'may cause crashes'.* https://fortune.com/2023/02/16/tesla-recalls-all-362758-vehicles-with-full-self-driving-beta-may-cause-crashes-ota-software-update-elon-musk/. 2023 (cited on page 126).

39   Matthew McAteer Yada Pruksachatkun and Subhabrata (Subho) Majumda. *Practicing Trustworthy Machine Learning.* https://learning.oreilly.com/library/view/practicing-trustworthy-machine/9781098120269/ch03.html. Feb. 2023 (cited on page 127).

40   *Jon Krohn.* 2022. url: https://www.jonkrohn.com/posts/2022/10/7/tedx-talk-how-neuroscience-inspires-ai-breakthroughs-that-will-change-the-world (cited on page 133).

41   ACM. *ACM TechBrief: Policies for Safer Algorithmic Systems Urgently Needed.* https://www.acm.org/media-center/2023/january/techbrief-safer-algorithmic-systems. 2023 (cited on page 135).

42   Netflix. *Cunk On Earth.* https://www.netflix.com/title/81516751. 2023 (cited on page 137).

43   The Economist. *AI-wielding tech firms are giving a new shape to modern warfare | The Economist.* https://www.economist.com/business/2023/02/16/ai-wielding-tech-firms-are-giving-a-new-shape-to-modern-warfare. Feb. 2023 (cited on page 137).

44   John Maynard Keynes, Elizabeth Johnson, and Donald Moggridge. *The Collected Writings of John Maynard Keynes (Volume 5).* Cambridge University Press, Dec. 2012 (cited on page 139).

45   John" "Le Carre. *"Tinker, Tailor, Soldier, Spy".* "Penguin Books", "June" 2011" (cited on page 139).

46   Gary Marcus. *Is chatgpt really a 'code red' for google search?* Jan. 2023. url: https://cacm.acm.org/blogs/blog-cacm/268376-is-chatgpt-really-a-code-red-for-google-search/fulltext (cited on page 141).

47   Steve Wozniak Elon Musk et al. *Pause Giant AI Experiments: An Open Letter - Future of Life Institute.* https://futureoflife.org/open-letter/pause-giant-ai-experiments/. 2023 (cited on page 147).